# BECOMING AN AMERICAN GUNSMITH

## Your Path To Personal Freedom And Financial Security

# BECOMING AN AMERICAN GUNSMITH

## Your Path To Personal Freedom And Financial Security

GENE WAYNE KELLY

This book is for Individuals who love freedom and firearms, and have the desire to become a Gunsmith.

American
Gunsmithing
Institute

To become a Certified Professional Gunsmith, contact:

American Gunsmithing Institute

351 Second Street, Napa, CA. 94559

1-800-797-0867

**www.AmericanGunsmithingInstitute.com**

For FREE Gunsmithing Mini lessons and
Video Armorer's Courses on your specific firearms, contact:
**www.AmericanGunsmith.com**

1-800-797-0867

To join a community of like minded individuals, go to:

The Gunsmithing Club of America

**www.GunsmithingClubofAmerica.com**

Gunsmithing Student Success Stories:

**www.AgiReviews.com**

# TABLE OF CONTENTS

## Introduction

# WELCOME TO MY GREATEST PASSION

I wrote this book to invite you to share in my Greatest Passion. *Gunsmithing!*

In this book I want you to realize that becoming a qualified Gunsmith is within your grasp. I also want to reveal to you how to acquire the basic "Must Have" knowledge needed to become successful as a Gunsmith.

Further, I want to invite you to join a Community of Gunsmiths and become part of America's Firearms Heritage and Legacy.

I started the American Gunsmithing Institute (AGI) to preserve the Gunsmithing Arts and to make them readily available to anyone who had the desire to pursue them.

Every gun has a story. But, without Gunsmiths the story would soon end. There would not be functioning firearms available to protect our freedoms, to Hunt, Target Practice, participate in competitions, or just collect and enjoy.

What ultimately defines AGI and the Gunsmithing Club of America is people just like you, who are in love with the idea of gunsmithing and want to personally keep the heritage of firearms craftsmanship alive.

The Gunsmithing Club of America's most important job, and one that we love doing year round is creating an environment for all of our students, Gunsmiths, instructors, graduates and firearm enthusiasts to come together to exchange information, share ideas and achieve the dream of making their passion into their livelihood.

As the founder and president of the American Gunsmithing Institute and the Gunsmithing Club of America, I want to keep inspiring everyone who is, has been, or will be a part of our world.

To do so, I will need to share a little bit about myself and what I think is important if you want to be a Successful Gunsmith.

I have written this book with all of that in mind. This book is, chapter by chapter, the embodiment of who I am and what I believe in. To my great joy, the size and dedication of the AGI Gunsmithing community has shown me that there are so many people who share my feelings.

It is certainly important to be able to earn money doing what you love and not dread your workday. If you love Guns, being a Gunsmith will certainly enable you to achieve that goal.

This book will help guide you on your personal path to becoming a Gunsmith. It is a great way to begin to immerse yourself in this special community . . . and if you are a gun-guy or gal, I hope that it will also be enjoyable reading!

I hope you enjoy what I have chosen to share with you. And I wish you fulfillment, freedom, and fun in all you do.

Sincerely,

Gene Wayne Kelly
President American Gunsmithing Institute
Gunsmithing Club of America

## Chapter One

# THE FIRST GUNSMITHS IN AMERICA

Firearms have been part of American history from the very beginning with the first successful settlements of Europeans on the North American continent, including the Pilgrims landing at Plymouth Rock.

I have personally viewed the oldest known firearm in America, a "Wheel Lock" rifle in the NRA Museum – It is a "Pilgrim Rifle" attributed to ownership by John Alden, one of the Pilgrim leaders of Plymouth Colony.

Alden, who embarked on the Mayflower as a 20-year-old cooper, joined Captain Miles Standish's militia to defend the settlers from outside attacks. The rifle was discovered hundreds of years later during restoration of the Alden Home in 1924. This wheel lock is typical of the rifles possessed by the early settlers of America.

Alden - Mayflower Wheel-lock, located in the NRA museum.

As the land was settled, Americans needed more firearms for hunting and to defend themselves. They also needed the firearms they owned repaired, so they turned to American's first gunsmiths.

For early settlers pioneering the wilderness of North America, gunsmiths became vital members of small settlements. These skilled metalsmiths developed the American long-rifle, which also became known as the Pennsylvania or Kentucky rifle. These rifles were sometimes elaborately carved and decorated with finely etched brass or silver plates. But the rifle's most critical quality was its extended barrel that featured twisting lands and grooves along the interior of the bore known as "rifling." These grooves made a lead ball, or other projectile, spin as it exited the barrel, stabilizing the bullet and ensuring greater accuracy. These guns were made by hand one at a time, which required a great deal of skill, time, and money.

During the Revolutionary War, some American militia fighters engaged in guerilla-style tactics using their hunting rifles to attack British soldiers from distant cover.

There were only a handful of gunsmiths in America in its first century and a half of settlement. The old method of becoming a gunsmith required an apprenticeship with a gunsmith. This included studying under them for ten to twenty years.

Gunsmithing is a trade with a truly distinguished past. The first firearms date back to the 1200s and were invented in China. This technology eventually made its way to Europe and Italian craftsmen assembled that continent's first gun barrels. I have personally handled a pistol with a barrel made by Beretta nearly 500 years ago.

In other parts of the world gunsmiths had to join a guild or union and follow their rules. But Americans are proud and independent, so they rejected the concept of having to ask others for permission to build things a certain way. The end result has been that Gunsmiths in America are far more innovative than many of their counterparts around the world, possibly because they aren't afraid to break the rules that were set by guilds. At the American Gunsmithing Institute, we are still breaking the rules today.

Being a gunsmith in the early years of gun-making in America demanded tremendous patience and knowledge. Indeed, making guns from raw materials (without the benefit of pre-made parts) required being proficient in several trades: specifically, woodworking, blacksmithing, and general metalworking, among others.

Most work was done by hand which meant it frequently took as long as 400 hours to produce a single rifle. To learn gunsmithing an apprentice toiled for many years under a master before striking out on their own. The Revolutionary War changed the way gunsmiths worked and the way the profession grew; gunsmiths had to create and produce firearms much faster and in larger quantities than they ever had before. This increase in demand helped to drive the American Industrial Revolution.

To boost the fledgling nation's home-grown arsenal, General George Washington ordered the establishment of the Springfield Armory in Springfield, Massachusetts, in 1776. Following the Revolutionary War, Congress also established Harpers Ferry Armory in West Virginia in 1798 to boost weapon and ammunition production.

Around the same time, the U.S. government and some states began hiring smaller gun-making outfits to produce guns or gun parts which could be used with the weapons being produced at the U.S. armories. Some of the oldest U.S. gun makers got their start at that time, including Eliphalet Remington, who began producing flintlock rifles in 1816.

The same Remington Arms Company has continued to manufacture firearms to this day. Eli Whitney, originally famous for inventing the cotton gin in the 1790s, developed a system to produce interchangeable rifle parts thanks to his winning a contract with the U.S. War Department to create 10,000 to 15,000 muskets in 1800. This was the very beginning of mass production of firearms.

Several other well-known American gunsmith-inventors propelled firearms technology forward. In 1836, Samuel Colt received a U.S. Patent for a handheld pistol that featured a multi-firing system based on a rotating cylinder with multiple chambers. Soon Colt's name would become synonymous with the revolver. Other improvements followed, including breechloading systems which allowed the gunner to load the weapon from the rear, rather than having to tamp the powder and bullet down from the gun's muzzle end. Rear-loading or breechloading systems developed by gun manufacturers, including Sharps, Maynard and Burnside, packed the projectile and powder together in a single, combustible cartridge. The system not only saved time, it also avoided exposing gun powder to wet conditions.

One of Colt's advertising slogans, "God created man, Sam Colt made them equal," would become legend to gun-lovers. The Civil War funded a new boom in firearm manufacturing and technology and saw the ushering in of the self-contain cartridge near the end of the war.

One of the most acclaimed Gunsmith and firearms designer in history was John Moses Browning. He began designing ground-breaking, lever action, pump, semi-auto, and full-auto fire-arms. Some of the systems he invented, such as the "long-recoil," "short-recoil," and gas-operated systems are still in use today.

Some of his best-known firearms include; the Browning A-5, the Winchester Model 97 and Model 12 Shotguns 1894 Winchester ".30-30", Colt's 1911 .45 Auto pistol, the Browning Automatic Rifle (BAR), 1919 Belt fed machinegun, and the M2 .50 caliber machine gun, which is still used by the U.S. Military around the world today.

These forefathers blazed a gunsmithing trail of freedom-minded innovation backed by the Second Amendment to the Constitution. Many proud and independent gunsmiths thrive in America today and rely on respected institutions, such as the American Gunsmithing Institute and the Gunsmithing Club of America, for the latest gunsmith-related training, news, and information.

## Chapter Two

# PRESERVING THE GUNSMITHING ARTS

I recently sat down to do an interview about my love for the art of gunsmithing and why I started The American Gunsmithing Institute. The best way for me to communicate the life changing opportunities and personal fulfillment, not to mention freedom, gunsmithing can bring to you is by sharing my passion for it. There is not anything I have ever encountered that can change someone's life for the better as quickly and completely as entering the firearms industry. Here is my story, which has already inspired so many people to find their own success stories in gunsmithing.

## How long have you been involved in this industry and how did you start AGI?

Well I have been working in the firearms industry since I was in my late teens. I started AGI in 1993 based upon seeing an increased demand for Gunsmiths in the firearms industry. I realized there was a growing need to train new gunsmiths on a faster and more efficient basis.

My Gunsmithing story starts after I graduated from Napa High School in 1975. After a year or so of going to College, I was still trying to find out what I wanted to do in life. Being a Gunsmith had been suggested to me by a former Napa High School welding shop teacher as he knew I had a huge interest in firearms. So, I went to Lassen College to check out the program and found out there was a four-year waiting list to get in. I was told by the senior instructor, Bob Dunlap, that if I was willing to come up that summer and try to challenge the course, I might be able to get in for the Fall program.

So, I did and worked from the moment they opened the shop in the morning until they kicked me out at night. Well, I did pass the test and was invited back to start that fall in 1977. I went through the entire 2 1/2 year program. After graduating, Bob asked me if I wanted to work for him in his Gunsmithing Shop, because in addition to teaching, he maintained a full-time gun shop, so I did.

I learned a lot working there, but because I had my girlfriend and family down in the San Francisco Bay Area, I eventually returned there and worked for another shop as a gunsmith.

After that I worked as a California Deputy Game Warden for a while and then started and operated several successful businesses, including a firearms accessories manufacturing company and a security company. During this time, I developed an expertise for creating training courses that were taught entirely on video. We found that they were very successful as teaching tools.

As I considered how to best preserve and teach a Gunsmithing Course on video, I knew the best person to teach it would be my college Gunsmithing instructor, my "Sensei" if you will, Master Gunsmith Robert "Bob" Dunlap. At that time Bob was still teaching at Lassen College Gunsmithing School.

I sat down with Bob and talked about his teaching method. I realized that none of his program had ever been written out, it was all in his head, he was getting ready to retire and all of this would be lost. Nobody else was capable or ready to take over teaching his Gunsmithing System. It was all going to disappear! I decided I just could not let that happen.

His method was unique because he taught Design, Function, and Repair. The theory is you cannot fix something unless you truly understand how it works. Anyone else is what we call a "part swapper", someone who just orders and installs parts until the problem magically goes away without really understanding the "Why" or "How" of fixing it. And, that is dangerous!

As students, when Bob gave us tests, they were oral exams in front of all the other students, so you just could not fake it. If he thought you did not fully know the answers, he would ask "oh, really? Well what else, what if this happens?" You really had to know how everything worked and that is what made us the cream of the crop in terms of new Gunsmiths. And that is the level of knowledge I wanted to provide to AGI students, but in an easy to learn, more accessible format, using video.

So, I convinced Bob to teach his entire method on video. We began documenting his design, function, and repair course working on weekends and it took over 2 years. It ended up being 168 hours of core design, function, and repair instruction in centerfire rifles, shotguns, pistols and rimfire rifles on video. Thus, the American Gunsmithing Institute was born in 1993. There was nothing like it at the time and there still is not a better, faster way to learn gunsmithing. Today we are still continuing to preserve gunsmithing knowledge through the addition of new courses.

The reason that I created AGI was I could see the huge need in the United States for gunsmiths. We have over 350 million firearms in this country and at any given time 10 to 20 percent of those are in some need of cleaning, repair, or customizing; I mean we are talking tens of millions of firearms that need work. Right Now!

There were a lot of gunsmiths after World War II. These people would now be in their 70s, 80s and even 90s and they have either passed on or retired. Gunsmithing programs were only offered at a couple of campus-based schools and most people could not afford to attend them so the number of gunsmiths was continuing to decline.

The first problem is, they could only have so many people in a class. Second, you had to give up your income, travel to some other place and go live there for two and half years. Very few people could afford to do that. So, here we had a growing need which put our freedoms at risk and the "sit in the classroom" style of slow learning was becoming outdated.

Using Bob's teaching methodology combined with the video techniques we developed, we created a unique teaching method. We have gone on to use this same method to teach people welding, machining, locksmithing and other trade skills. So, that's kind of how the whole thing got started.

## What are some of the changes you have seen in the field of guns and Gunsmithing over the time you have been involved?

I think the entire firearms industry has changed a lot over the years. It has certainly grown into a multi-billion-dollar industry. However, the main designs of the firearms themselves have not changed all that much. There have been a few significant material and cosmetic changes such as with the Glock, and other polymer framed firearms. But not much has changed to the mechanisms used.

But, things have certainly changed in the Gunsmithing arena, Qualified Gunsmiths are in demand and are making more money. There have also been changes in the way people learn, and I think we have helped that change along. Because of the video revolution, people can now learn through distance education. They can learn about Gunsmithing at home, in their spare time, when they want to. This allows more people to get into the industry.

In addition, the Internet has obviously changed things because there is a lot more information available. Some of it is erroneous, but some of it is very good. This allows for lightning fast research to find the different things you need in the way of information, parts, and tools. So, I would say the delivery method of information in general has been the biggest change in the industry. The actual work we do, other than the materials, has not changed that much.

## Do some of those changes seem more obvious or dramatic in their impact in recent years?

Well, I don't know that I would call it dramatic, again except for our teaching style. There had previously been other home study courses, all of them were taught with little booklets, paper and ink, and quite honestly if you purchased a couple of different subscriptions to gun magazines or read a couple of really good Gunsmithing books you would have gotten the same information. Those courses are shallow and pretty lame.

The dramatic change was the American Gunsmithing Institute (AGI) bringing professional level, step by step, video instruction to the marketplace. You know we say a picture's worth a thousand words, well then moving pictures with words are worth tens of thousands. Trying to explain something in a book, like how to move a spring under the leg of this particular arm and hook it into here and so on with this amount of tension, is just very difficult to do. But on video we can show and tell you exactly how to do it.

Most people these days are not efficient and effective readers of technical data. But almost everyone knows how to learn by watching somebody do something, by watching video and hearing them describe what they are doing. So, the most dramatic change other than the access to parts and other information on the internet has been our delivery of a video instructional process and home study.

## You seem to have a real passion for preserving the trades. Where do you think that passion spawned?

I have a really strong belief in this country, what the founders of this country intended and the opportunity they created. I have a lot of respect for people who have served and protected the country to allow us to keep these different freedoms. And, I think if we do not preserve this information, a major portion of our freedoms are in jeopardy.

Specifically, if firearms cannot be repaired, having 350 million of them is of little value to the American people. Firearms do many things, not only do they protect the country, they protect through our law enforcement personnel, they protect individuals in their homes, they provide for recreation, they provide for the continuing of the traditions of hunting, collecting, or target shooting.

## What are 3 recommendations you would have for someone considering pursuing Gunsmithing as a profession?

1. **Decide whether they want to do this as a hobby or a profession.** If they want to pursue Gunsmithing as a hobby, meaning they are not so worried about "How am I going to make money at this," that is one fork in the road. It will determine to a degree what you end up studying. Even as

a hobby, it is quite probable you are going to want professional level knowledge. Most of us, when we pursue a hobby, want to do it well. But at that point you are not under any pressure to create a financially successful venture.

If you are going to do this professionally, you need to look at not just the learning of the trade itself. That is where many people get focused as technicians, they only want to learn the technical aspect. But, they also need to become aware of what it takes to operate a successful business. That is one of the reasons we have done so much in providing our students with educational material in that area. Real world, not just books, this is stuff I have learned over 30 years of running successful businesses. That is recommendation number one.

❷ **Look at your learning style and ask yourself, "how do I learn best?"** Can I learn only by sitting in a classroom, the way I was taught in school, or do I actually learn better by watching videos, at home, doing what I've been shown and being able to refer back to what I've seen as many times as necessary? The footnote to that is speed. I believe in speed.

As you probably know, regular classes are usually taught at the speed of the slowest learner in the class. But our programs do not punish anybody. I believe in Speed Learning, so if you're capable of completing the course in 90 days, going through all the material and understanding it, and completing the certification tests, then you should be able to do that.

On the other hand, if you are someone who does not have the time to focus and it is going to take two years to do the same thing, then you should be able to do that too. My point is that you set the pace, do not let some teaching style that is structurally limited set it for you.

Classrooms are very limited in the teaching methods they can support and often times if you do not have enough students in the class, the class is canceled. Many of us experienced that in college. Then you don't get it this semester and you have to wait till next semester. So, look at your learning style and find out what works for you. Do not be sold a bill of goods that you have to go to some campus, spend a couple of years and learn at the slowest pace.

There is an old outdated mentality in the Trades that only slow learning over 4 years of being an apprentice or something like that allows you to be competent. Competent people are competent people. The incompetent will never become competent. So why learn slowly when you can learn fast?

**❸ Look in your pocketbook.** You need to say to yourself, OK, based on my finances, what route can I afford to go. How can I afford to do this? I find that if people ask themselves "How can I" instead of just saying "I can't", they will find the answers. If they want to go to a campus-based school they need to be prepared to spend two-plus years there, cover tuition and living expenses, and suffer without their normal income. All of these factors need to be considered, and if that's the way you learn best and you are financially able, great.

But if instead they want to learn at the fastest speed possible, if they want to do it at home so that they do not have to give up their job and be away from their family, if they want to do it at a fraction of the cost of a campus based school, then they really need to seek out distance education. And, on the distance education side, I invite them to look at every other course offered and they will find that AGI's is the only course that offers the design, function, and repair training technique, let alone many of the customizing techniques, and add on materials, as well as the extended skills such as machining and welding. It is also the only course taught entirely on video. Also, no other school provides them the high level instruction we do in the area of business skills needed to be successful.

21

Those are three great suggestions Gene, let me ask you this . . .

## What do you think separates a true gunsmith from a "part-swapper"?

A true gunsmith is able to analyze a system, determine what is wrong and make the repair, often with the existing parts. That means if a part is broken, they can weld it, fit it, and fix it. They can shape a new part, they can heat treat when needed, and, whatever they put in there will function safely and properly.

On the other hand, a part swapper doesn't understand exactly how the systems work. He can see that maybe this part or that part is broken, orders a new part, puts it in and now it still does not work.

Why? Because there are tolerance variations from the parts that are manufactured at the factories. That is why they are fitted. Or maybe you have some wear on another part, now you've put in a brand-new part and the relationship between the old part and new part is such that it is still out of time or not properly operating.

So, what a part swapper will do, and I've seen a lot of these guys that call themselves "gunsmiths", they will reach in the parts bin, get the next part and try that one, until they find something that works. That is not professional Gunsmithing. A professional gunsmith is able to look at the system, even one that they may have never seen before, analyze how the system works, and from there make the appropriate repair. And that is exactly what our design function and repair course teaches.

## You have been successful in many different businesses. What training or experiences from your earlier days in Gunsmithing do you feel have helped you to accomplish these successes?

I think one of the most important things does not come from just Gunsmithing itself. It comes from a personal philosophy. That philosophy is wrapped up in the red white and blue Americana I believe in. Maybe I watched too many westerns when I was a kid or read too many books, but I really do believe that you do not ever quit.

It is also smart to cut smart corners, meaning do not learn at the slowest pace, learn at the fastest pace. There is no extra benefit given by taking a long time to learn something. People do not care and they certainly do not give you more interest on the money you put in the bank whether or not it took you a long time to earn it or a short time. I believe in Speed. Speed learning, speed earning.

Some of the other traits I have in addition to being very tenacious, is being able to step back and look at the whole project. A lot of people get myopic in the way they look at things, every once in a while, you've got to step back and "say what am I trying to accomplish here."

That is one of the things that has helped me be very successful in my relationships with customers of all types, whether in the security industry or Gunsmithing. Another skill is asking the right questions. Rather than focusing on just what they say, this is wrong or this is the problem or this is what I want done, step back and say "How do you plan on using this?", "What do you want to accomplish?", "What is the result that you are looking for"?

When you take that kind of approach and a bigger view of things, you then make sure you go down the right path. Otherwise, you may immediately select the wrong path and hit a dead end, then nobody is happy. I apply these techniques every day in business.

## For someone considering a Gunsmithing career, what do your courses offer that is different?

I would say there are a number of things, and I'm going to start with number one, Master Gunsmith Bob Dunlap. Bob developed AGI's Professional Gunsmithing Course curriculum and was the original instructor. This is the complete Design, Function, and Repair course. His philosophy of how to go about the teaching of design, function, and repair, how he demonstrates it and makes it so clear is what makes us special. So, number one is really Bob and his teaching style.

Number two is obviously what we bring to the table with our video production skills. Showing close ups that you could not see from the front of the classroom, let alone the back. Here you are just inches away, seeing everything up close, which leads to visual understanding, and comprehension.

Third, I would say that ALL our other instructors are real world gunsmiths. They are not just teachers. Even though Bob spent a lot of time teaching college, he simultaneously maintained a full-time professional gunsmithing shop, with up to 10 gunsmiths working for him. He has seen such an incredible number of different and complicated repairs.

Every one of our instructors, learned what they are teaching not out of a textbook or out of a classroom or from creating a lesson plan. They're teaching from real-world experience based on thousands of hours of learning the hard way, so that our students don't have to.

## How prepared are the graduates?

Very prepared, our testing process is purposefully difficult. The reason we do that is we want to make sure our students really understand how things work. Therefore, our written testing is meant to maintain a high bar, so when our students graduate, they are going to know how Firearms Systems really work. Our students are so prepared, and our certifications are so well respected in the industry, that, in fact, there are some companies that will only hire AGI graduates.

Students also have the ability to go back and watch the videos as often as they want. This is a huge benefit because my understanding is you retain less than 12% of what you learn in the classroom, and I can tell you that the older you get it's probably a whole lot less than that. AGI students have a video library to use as reference material anytime they need!

## Can you tell me about your Business Program?

Well, with our Master Gunsmith course we offer a Business Success Package. Included in that package are audio interviews with various instructors explaining how they handle the work flow, tips they use in the shops that help them work more efficiently. Some of their background stories help illuminate how they got to be so successful.

We include a marketing manual to help the student or business owner market their business successfully. We created an 11 CD series called "The Business Success Toolbox" that is essentially a "mini -MBA program," based on my many business successes. It was created by me and April Palmer, a business coach who has worked with over 500 businesses of all varieties.

You need to understand how to create goals, how to get things done, time management, how to handle your finances, how to market, how to attract business and so on. All of that is covered, PLUS . . .

. . . we created something exciting, the industry's first flat rate manual. Just like the automotive industry's flat rate manual, this shows you how to price a particular job based upon an Industry Standard of number of hours to perform that job, multiplied by your shop labor rate.

Let us say for example you wanted to put a recoil pad on a double gun and the manual says you get 1.5 hours for that, you would multiply 1.5 times your shop rate. We usually recommend the shop rate be somewhere in the neighborhood of 50 to 80 percent of what the local automotive shops charge because the average automotive shops have a much higher overhead than you do.

Here in our area, automotive shops are about $90 to $120 per hour for automotive services. So, if you took a rate of $100, half of that would be $50 an hour. So, let's work with that figure. In this example you would calculate 1.5 times that, or $75.00, and that would be what you charge. By showing the customer this flat rate book, it just takes away all the doubt, and confers legitimacy; after all it is printed and national.

There are other tools as well in the business success package including how to get your Federal Firearms License and a lot of other material.

## How does your personal philosophy apply to where you are going with AGI?

Well a big part of my passion and role here has been to preserve knowledge, not just for Gunsmithing, but for all the trades in general. That is why we have also created courses for other related trades such as Machining and Welding.

I equate knowledge about how to do things with personal freedom. They say knowledge is power and I agree completely. Applicable knowledge is even more powerful. So, people who are not able to do mechanical things are kind of handicapped in a way.

We have a whole generation of people who can do wonderful things on the computer and I think that is great, but they cannot do anything mechanical. We have even more people who spend their entire life moving paper from one pile to another, and they are very frustrated internally because they really do not know how to "do" anything. I've heard it said, "You know my dad was a mechanic, he made parts on a machine, and I've got dad's old lathe in the garage and I don't even know how to turn it on."

Rather than let all of this knowledge slip away, our first priority is to preserve it, then teach it in such a way that people can learn it quickly. That is, not taking the four or eight years it took to learn a skill back in the old days. Now with our courses it only requires days and weeks to learn these same skills. I like to say, "we are turning decades into days."

Then they can apply these skills to their own ends, wherever they are, whatever industry or situation that they are in, that is what we are about. To me it all boils down to personal freedom, but you have to take the step of saying "I'm responsible individually for teaching and improving myself."

The "Three Musketeers of Lassen College Gunsmithing School," 40 years later. L-R; Mark Foster (Gunsmith, Master Armorer and AGI Instructor), Gene Kelly (Gunsmith, Founder & President of the American Gunsmithing Institute) and Darrell Holland (Master Gunsmith, President Holland's Shooters Supply and AGI Instructor).

Do not wait for somebody else to do it, do not wait for somebody else to hand it to you or fund it. Choose to do what you want to do, get the knowledge you need, then move on creating your own personal success.

Become an American Gunsmith.

Go to: **www.AmericanGunsmithingInstitute.com**

## Chapter Three

# HOW I ALMOST DESTROYED MY DAD'S BOSS' HEIRLOOM SHOTGUN!

I am going to share a story with you about how I almost destroyed my dad's boss' heirloom shotgun but managed to bring it back from the dead. I am telling it to illustrate two very important concepts. The first is that none of us knows what he or she is doing without sufficient training. The second lesson is that even when all seems lost, if you've got the right tools, know-how and confidence you will probably come out just fine.

When I was in gunsmithing school, and relatively new at it, my dad's boss asked him if I could fix the old '97 Winchester pump shotgun he had been using for years and that he had gotten from his father. Of course I willingly accepted the job and was excited to work on it. This shotgun had been used hard and put away wet. All the finish was worn off the gun and the buttstock had repairs on it with the toe of the stock broken off and a piece of broomstick nailed on to replace it. Overall the gun was a wreck, but it functioned and it was my dad's boss' favorite hunting gun.

In preparing to blue it, I stripped the gun all the way down. A Winchester '97 has two cartridge stops with cartridge release buttons coming through the side of the receivers on some models; one of the cartridge-stops came out fine. The other cartridge-stop had the screw head, which is a fine, threaded long screw with half of it being a pin that the cartridge stop pivoted on. It was only about an eighth of an inch in diameter. Unfortunately, half the head of the screw slot was broken off, so trying to do the right thing I knew I needed to remove it. It was suggested to me that I could drill it out. So, I set it up in a machine vice in a drill press and attempted to drill out the screw. When I took it out of the vice, I was horrified to see that the drill had flexed slightly as it was drilling and had come out the side of the receiver! I was looking at a hole in the side of the receiver that I had just drilled in my dad's boss' heirloom shotgun.

I was absolutely horrified! What was I going to do? At first, I had no idea but did know I needed help. I knew a guy who was very good at TIG welding and I had him TIG weld the hole in the side of the receiver, which I then reshaped both inside and out to original dimensions. I then prepped the receiver by sanding, filing and bluing the receiver, the barrel and all the appropriate metal parts. I then refinished the stocks replacing the piece of broomstick with a piece of walnut that I blended into the rest of the stock and buttstock. I refinished both the fore-end and the buttstock with a clear Varathane style finish after staining the wood to a beautiful walnut color. I also installed a new recoil pad and fitted it. The whole gun looked better than new.

When my father presented his boss with the shotgun, he was absolutely amazed and couldn't believe it was the same firearm he had given me. His words of praise were very gratifying, and he never knew how close to disaster I had come!

What it taught me was there's really nothing you cannot fix. No disaster that you cannot overcome when you are working as a gunsmith. That disaster ended up giving me a lot of confidence. What you need to be able to do is take on every project with total confidence, knowing you too, as a certified design, function, and repair gunsmith, will be able to figure out how to repair it.

There are some guns that are not safe to put back into use for a variety of reasons but 99% of the time if you needed to, you would be able to fix them. So, to be a real gunsmith, you have to be willing to risk actually having something go very badly, even risk damaging a firearm in the process of learning, but take heart. There is virtually always a way out. We teach our students at the American Gunsmithing Institute not only how to remove metal, but how to put it back using TIG welding and other techniques. We also teach you how to repair stocks and blend and colorize them along with refinishing them to make them look better than new. They are often capable of duplicating original finishes.

Working on my dad's boss' shotgun could have ended in absolute embarrassment and disaster, but because I had Design, Function, and Repair training, having learned gunsmithing from master gunsmith Robert "Bob" Dunlap, I had the confidence to tackle my problem head on.

Again, the sweetest victories are the ones taken from the mouth of defeat. Be bold, courageous, and gunsmith without fear. You can fix anything!

Join the Gunsmithing Club of America and we will help you succeed. **www.GunsmithingClubOfAmerica.com**

## Chapter Four

# WHO IS A GUNSMITH?

A gunsmith is a person who repairs, modifies, designs, or builds guns. The occupation differs from an armorer, who usually replaces only worn parts in standard firearms.

Gunsmiths can now do modifications and changes to a firearm that it used to take several years of training and practical experience under a higher-level gunsmith, attendance at a gunsmithing school, or both. But not now, not with the accelerated training from the American Gunsmithing Institute.

Gunsmiths also do factory level repairs and renovations to restore much used or deteriorated firearms to new condition. They may make alterations to adapt sporting guns to better fit the individual shooter that may require extensive modifications to the firearms' stocks and metal parts. The repairs and redesigns may require fabrication and fitting of non-available parts and assemblies, which the gunsmith usually fabricates himself.

Gunsmiths may also renew metal finishes to new condition levels or apply carvings, engravings, and other decorative features to an otherwise-finished gun. The environment in which all of that takes place often varies depending on the specific locality, with some gun stores featuring one or a handful of individuals performing this work under their roof, some may work as individuals in their own, separate shop, or it may be a group of highly-trained specialist craftspeople who each contribute their individual skill to completely manufacture highly-crafted custom made firearms from basic metal and wood raw materials.

A gunsmith is really a renaissance man. It is useful to possess skills as a parts fabricator, a metalworker or blacksmith, a wood-worker and an artisan; be knowledgeable in shop mathematics, ballistics, chemistry, and materials engineering; be knowledgeable in the use and application of a variety of hand, power, and machinists tools and measuring devices; and be capable of working accurately and precisely. The American Gunsmithing Institute teaches you all of this.

The AGI course covers all aspects of handguns in detail.

Those who are self-employed in small gunsmith shops must also possess skills as small business operators; work effectively with a wide variety of customers; and remain abreast of, and comply with federal, state, and local laws, ordinances, and requirements.

Gene personally teaching an AGI Gunsmithing Student aspects of the Browning A-5 Long Recoil Shotgun during optional one week intensive hands-on classes for AGI alumni students.

Due to the great breadth of subject matter to be mastered, many gunsmiths specialize in only a few of the skills required of the general gunsmith. Alternatively, some gunsmiths learn many of the skills of the trade, but only apply them to a few weapon types (e.g. only pistols, only shotguns, only specific brands or models). They require a firm grasp of the knowledge of Design, Function, and Repair. The primary *technical* responsibility of gunsmiths is to ensure that the guns work and function safely.

They accomplish this first by always properly observing and demonstrating gun safety, in their handling procedures: both in their own actions, and in the actions of their customers and the people around them.

They accomplish this secondly by inspecting guns to ensure safe mechanical operation. Gunsmiths use their in-depth knowledge of guns to guide these inspections: either repairing deficiencies; or notifying customers of unsafe conditions and taking steps to prevent catastrophic failures.

Some of the conditions a Gunsmith looks for when inspecting a firearm brought to them for repairs are:

- Improper Assembly

- Missing Parts

- Cracks: all cracked parts are cause for concern, but especially so in the chamber-area, bolt, bolt-lugs, or buttstock.

- Bore Obstructions: being either dented or bent barrels, or foreign material in barrels.

- Improper Headspace: dimensions concerning the relative locations of the chamber and the bolt are not within specified tolerances.

- Improper Timing: (applies to full automatic firearms and revolvers,)

- Safety-Mechanism Malfunctions: potentially allowing a gun with the safety mechanism supposedly engaged to unexpectedly fire.

- Worn Sear Edges: potentially allowing a firearm to unexpectedly fire when the safety mechanism is disengaged.

- Firing-Pin Tips Deformed: leading to the possibility of primer-rupture.

This list is not comprehensive. Many failure modes are dependent on the particular model of firearm.

**Typical Gunsmithing Jobs include:**

- Disassemble, clean, inspect, lubricate & reassemble.

- Remove corrosion and touch-up finish.

- Repair burred or damaged parts with files & stones.

- Replace defective parts with factory-made replacements, hand-fitting as necessary.

- Add after-market customizations:

  - sling-swivels

  - recoil-pads

  - iron-sights

  - scopes

  - grip caps

  - butt plates

- Repair and re-finish wooden stock parts.

- Checker or re-checker grip areas.

- Deepen or clean up worn or damaged engravings and markings.

- Re-crown damaged muzzles on a lathe.

- Repair dented shotgun barrels.

- Install (solder) or repair rib on shotgun barrels, or repair double-barrel assemblies.

- Measure & correct head-space dimensions.

- Check for excessive bore erosion.

- Troubleshoot and repair feeding, ejecting, and firing problems.

- Test-fire guns with conventional loads to ensure proper operation.

- Fabricate wooden stocks to customer specifications and body dimensions. Fit same to existing receiver and barrel.

- Glass-bed actions to stocks to improve accuracy.

- Remove existing metal finish, and re-blue metal parts.

- Fabricate replacement parts from metal stock.

- Modify trigger-pull weight through careful stoning of trigger mechanism parts.

- Fire "proof-loads" through weapons to ensure sufficient strength of parts under over-load conditions.

- Replace worn barrels, which have fired so many rounds that they are no longer of the specified caliber (which leads to loss of accuracy).

- Change caliber or cartridge of existing rifle, by changing barrel, and modifying receiver.

- Re-cut rifling and change caliber of existing barrel.

- Design and build complete rifles by fitting stock barrels to stock receivers; fabricating or purchasing additional parts as needed, and fitting same to rifle.

- Design and build a complete rifle, shotgun, or combination gun from start to finish.

Combination guns, usually referred to as a "drilling", is a highly complex hand-made long gun with several joined barrels combining both rifle and shotgun calibers and gauges sharing a common breech and buttstock.) The highest level examples of custom-made firearms usually start out as several pieces of blank steel stock or rough forged parts, a slab (stock blank) of walnut; steel tubes with rifled or smooth holes ("bores") drilled their length, and are usually hand made by highly skilled gunsmiths using nothing more than an occasional lathe, milling machine, heat treating furnace (for making springs, hardening parts to the proper hardness, and color case hardening) with the majority of roughing, fitting, and finishing done completely by hand using files, scrapers, abrasive paper and cloth, chisels and rasps.

While some gunsmiths are general practitioners in this trade, some of the more important specializations are:

**Custom builder/designer:** Builds guns to customer's specification, from raw materials and shelf parts. Gunsmiths specializing in custom areas can be called upon by professional target-shooters, avid sports shooters, or anyone that wants custom attributes added to their firearm to create highly accurate or custom looking firearms.

A Custom Gunsmith also builds high-end firearms for hunters and shooters with needs and desires that cannot be served by standard catalogued firearms offered by gun manufacturers. They may work in partnership with engravers and other specialized artists to produce unique finishes and decorations not possible on regular mass-produced firearms.

Some highly specialized gunsmiths can complete all firearm modifications without anyone else in the industry helping them. This is likely the most highly skilled of gunsmiths, as they are required not only to have proficiency in the other areas of gunsmithing, but must also be well educated in firearm finishing and machining, in order to manufacture the individual components and even springs before assembly takes place.

Gunsmiths are skilled tradespeople who design, build, modify, renovate and repair firearms of all sorts. They may also engage in creative work, such as metal engraving and woodcarving. The duties of gunsmiths vary by specialization and employer. The majority of gunsmiths are self-employed; however, they may also be employees of firearms manufacturers, the military and law-enforcement agencies, gun shops and sporting goods stores.

Because the general duties of gunsmiths are so broad, they must possess or acquire a wide range of skills, including all of the following:

- A complete understanding of Firearms Systems Design, Function, and Repair.

- Metalworking Capabilities

- Welding, primarily Gas & TIG

- Woodworking

- Parts fabrication

- Basic Mathematics

Gunsmiths must be proficient in using several types of tools in order to perform their duties adequately. In addition to using hand tools, most gunsmiths must use basic power tools and machinist tools. Finally, gunsmiths have to stay abreast of all local and federal laws pertaining to firearms. These laws may change frequently, and they may be very complex or difficult to understand.

## Duties and Responsibilities of a Gunsmith

The overriding responsibility of a gunsmith is to ensure that the firearms he or she is working on operate safely and according to specifications. No matter what specific process they are engaged in at the moment, gunsmiths must observe safe gun-handling procedures and ensure that customers, assistants and coworkers do the same.

All of the mechanisms of the guns must be inspected for safety, and any deficiencies must be fixed before the job can commence or continue. Following are just a few of the reasons why guns may be unsafe even when handled properly:

| | |
|---|---|
| Assembled incorrectly | Improperly aligned |
| Parts missing | Timing problems |
| Cracks and other damage | Excessive wear and tear |
| Obstructions | Firing pin deformities |

## Common Tasks Performed by Gunsmiths

Following are some of the most common tasks that gunsmiths may be called on to perform:

| |
|---|
| Assemble and dissemble firearms |
| Inspect, clean, and lubricate firearms |
| Remove corrosion from metal gun parts |
| Repair damaged guns |
| Add custom or aftermarket parts, such as swivels, recoil pads, sights, scopes, grips, and stocks. |
| Repair or refinish wooden handles, grips, and stocks |
| Touch up engravings and other markings |
| Fit barrels |
| Remove dents |
| Correct headspace of guns and cartridges |
| Replace barrels and firing mechanisms |
| Modify pull weight and other trigger mechanisms |

## Gunsmith Specializations

Most gunsmiths are generalists and deal with duties as they are presented, but others focus on one of several specializations, which may call for specific tasks to be completed. A few of the most common specializations are as follows:

- **Custom manufacturer** – A custom manufacturer designs and builds unique firearms according to a customer's specifications or desires. In order to complete jobs, custom gunsmiths may use stock parts or raw materials, which requires advanced machining skills.

- **Finisher** – Once a firearm has been manufactured and assembled, it requires some degree of finishing. Finishing jobs may including Parkerizing, bluing, browning and case hardening.

- **Stockmaker** – Stockmakers specialize in fitting wood to metal by carving rifle stocks, shotgun stocks and pistol grips from one of several species of wood, including walnut, maple and birch. In order to be successful in this specialization, stockmakers must be proficient in using saws, files, chisels and other woodworking tools.

- **Engraver** – Many pistols and rifles are exquisitely engraved with patterns or pictures. This work requires a steady hand and the ability to use pneumatic engraving systems or hand engravers.

But, the one aspect ALL of these specialized Gunsmiths MUST possess is a strong understanding of Design, Function, and Repair (DF&R), otherwise modifications they make to a firearm could result in an un-safe condition.

*Sources for this chapter: personal experience, wikipedia and the internet.*

## Chapter Five

# GUNSMITHING: THE ROAD TO FINANCIAL FREEDOM

### "Are You Prepared for the New Retirement Reality?"

Instead of the traditional employment on/off switch — work full-time and then full stop, growing numbers of people are earning an income well into their traditional retirement years, typically embracing part-time and flexible work. *As a society we have to get serious about encouraging people to stay in the labor force longer and have longer careers,"* says Jeffrey Brown, economist and dean of the College of Business at the University of Illinois at Urbana- Champaign.

Being prepared for that "rainy day" is just common sense. And make no mistake . . . the economy can turn on a dime, from good to bad or from bad to even worse! Plus, if you are counting on Social Security to keep your retirement afloat, the foundation for your future is built atop very thin ice indeed. According to Investopedia, it's been estimated that the "money" in Social Security's bank account will essentially run dry in 2035 — at which point it will only have 77% of what it's obligated to pay out that year. Unless Washington DC gets its act together to come up with some kind of solution (like that will ever happen), what this means in very real terms to YOU is that the benefits you may be counting on are more than likely to be slashed or even worse, vanish like the wind.

So, if you are currently retired, or can see it on the not-so-distant horizon, getting started earning even a part-time income in the traditional retirement years can make a *big difference* to your household finances. For example, bringing home $20,000 in part-time earnings is equivalent to **not** having to withdraw 4% from a $500,000 retirement savings plan. (4% is a rule-of-thumb withdrawal rate in the personal finance industry.)

In addition to Gunsmithing, the skills you will learn, through the Master Gunsmithing course, you will learn systems analysis, machining, welding and general business skills that are applicable to numerous other businesses and business opportunities.

## You do not want to run out of money and not have the ability to earn more during your lifetime.

However, let us say you are not planning on retiring any time soon... you have a good job and it is going just fine. Everything is great, right? . . . But . . .

## What Would Happen If Your Employer Told You Tomorrow, "We Don't Need You Anymore"?

If you watch the news you have no doubt heard grumblings of another recession. Companies are always looking for ways to cut costs and some consumers are already tightening their wallets. Bureaucrats are campaigning to try and keep RAISING TAXES which would further devastate the economy. The United States debt has soared to TWENTY-ONE TRILLION DOLLARS and, at some point, that chicken has got to come home to roost. When it does, it will not be pretty. But having your own Gunsmithing business is one way to help insulate you from these threats.

Don't forget - it's almost a sure bet that over the next decade thousands if not millions of jobs will get replaced by robots and automation – and not just "burger flipping," but quality jobs that pay good wages – trucking, accounting, management, and more.

So, when it comes to finding work – especially given the very real prejudice against "seasoned" workers (ageism in the workplace, even though illegal, is a very common and very painful reality) – the prospects do not look as rosy as they might seem.

That's why it is wise to develop skills that a) cannot get outsourced overseas, b) cannot be done by some computer programmed machine, and c) fills a very real need that is not going away. And when it comes to choosing another source of income, you can't go wrong with one as in demand and as lucrative as Gunsmithing. Why?

Because one place people just do not scrimp on, good economy or bad, is their firearms. You will find that people who own them absolutely know they are important to keep in tip-top shape and to get fixed immediately when needed. Plus, they all love to have their guns customized.

They will stop going to movies, cut back on eating out at restaurants, cut vacations short – but there always seems to be money in the budget for firearms. If currently you *only have one source of income*, do not let yourself get blindsided and stranded without creating another source of income. Gunsmithing can be a great additional source... and, I think once you get into it, you will probably tell your boss "it's been a pleasure" and exit stage left to go do Gunsmithing full-time instead.

## 25,000 Gunsmiths Needed . . . But Fewer Than 5,000 Gunsmiths Exist, So You Are Sorely Needed and Will Be Highly appreciated!

With well over 300 million firearms in private hands in the United States today, with Millions more being manufactured every year, the need for gunsmiths is huge and will remain so for a very, very long time!

Let us do the math. If in any given year at least 10% of the guns (one out of 10) need: basic cleaning, repairs or customization, then there are at least 30 Million guns that need some sort of Gunsmithing done every year. You can see that there is an incredible need and market for Trained, Competent Certified Gunsmiths. Heck, I know that at least 10% of my guns need some sort of cleaning, repair work or customizing that I would like to do to them, what about yours? If you take that 30-Million-gun number and divide it by an average of 1200 guns repaired or customized per Gunsmith per year, it will require over 25,000 Gunsmiths just to maintain the current yearly need. But currently there are far fewer than 5,000 full-time Gunsmiths total nationwide. And many of those have never been properly trained & certified.

Then, when you take into account what the Government is attempting . . . even more regulation and stricter gun control laws, the need for Gunsmiths just increases because the average age of firearms increases, thus they need more gunsmithing. And, as gun sales soar with this threat, more gunsmiths are needed to service all the new guns. Gunsmiths are in the unique position that they win either way!

The Supreme Court has repeatedly defended the Second Amendment. As much as certain politicians would LOVE to confiscate firearms, they will not be able to . . . legally or otherwise. Firearms have been a stable part of American life since the Revolution and they will continue to be so. Gunsmiths will always be needed and valued by the public.

## So, we have a HUGE vacuum to fill – at least 20,000 are needed!

Are you able to rise to the occasion and help meet this need in our country and preserve our freedoms, while you make money Part-time, Full-Time or as a Retirement Income, Gunsmithing? Will you be One of the Few that receive the absolute best training in the world from the American Gunsmithing Institute?

## "How Much Can I REALLY Earn as a Gunsmith?"

As far as I know there is no other opportunity like this with such a low investment to get started...As an example one of the best franchise opportunities (I'm not going to name it but it's the #1 rated sandwich shop franchise) requires an investment of between $116,000 and $213,000 to open a single store. Most owners are ECSTATIC to earn $57k per year off that investment. And, they will have the headaches associated with managing numerous employees, the occasional irate or rude customer and the inevitable crises that come with owning such a business.

The more popular haircutting franchises will require a similar investment for about the same return. Not to mention you will be required to have a net worth of $300-500k, great credit and $150,000 or so in liquid assets. All of that investment expense to *maybe* make $50,000 or so a year.

But the worst part is . . . You do not even get to follow your REAL PASSION: Working on GUNS! Because if you love guns, love hunting, love the Second Amendment and why it matters, then you'll love Gunsmithing... an extremely rewarding and satisfying career, either part-time, full-time, running your own shop or working with someone else.

You can set up a basic gunsmithing shop for just a few thousand dollars. All you need to get started are some hand tools and a couple of common power tools. You do not need a complete machine shop as some people would have you believe...

And it is a real skill, a real career – earnings of $30-$50 per hour are not unusual for a skilled craftsman and some charge as much as $100 per hour. Here is a sample of some of the most common gunsmithing services and average fees charged by gunsmiths (these rates normally DO NOT include parts). In 2020:

| | |
|---|---|
| Routine troubleshooting | $25 - $75 |
| Detail Strip Cleaning | $35 - $65 |
| Smooth and Tune revolver | $65 - $95 |
| Tuning accuracy | $85 - $190 |
| Sight Installation | $85 - $190 |
| Swivel Installation | $15-$30 |
| Choke Installation | $90 - $190 |
| Recoil Pad Installation | $50 - $95 |
| Patterning a shotgun | $50 - $90 |
| Bedding a barreled action | $50 - 150 |
| Repairs to receiver | $50 - $100 |
| Repairing firing pin | $25-$55 |
| Trigger assembly/repair | $50 - $90 |
| Fitting a new trigger | $45 - $90 |
| Repair safety | $25 - $50 |

As you can see, it can add up fast – and if you are like me (and most gun owners), it'll hardly seem like work at all. You are tearing stuff apart, fixing it, and putting it back together. You will be getting paid good money to have FUN!

A part-time gunsmith, taking on side jobs on nights or weekends, can make an extra $10,000 to $20,000 or more per year pretty easily.

Taking it a little further (and we are NOT making any promises), someone working fulltime as a Gunsmith running their own shop, can make $50,000 a year, and if they are a bit more ambitious, operating a full-service shop, can even crack six figures... raking in as much as $120,000 per year! And that would only require working on 100 guns a month at $100 average per gun!

But, there is even more to it.

## No other business offers the flexibility and freedom that Gunsmithing provides.

Imagine deciding when you want to work and when you want to relax. Want to go on vacation, Hunting, or take a random day off? With Gunsmithing you have the freedom to decide how much work you want to take on and when to do it... if you have a family vacation planned you simply schedule the incoming jobs to be due before or after your vacation time.

And, it will be a REAL vacation. You will not be worried about what is going on at work or if your boss is mad at you or if layoffs are coming.

Want to take Friday afternoon off? Work a little faster during the week or arrange your schedule so nothing is due on that day. You have FULL control of your own life and financial destiny and peace of mind. You make the rules!

If you think about all of the things you do not like about your current situation, you can begin to imagine just how the flexibility and extra income provided by Gunsmithing will give you more freedom, make your life easier, and offer the security of knowing you have a skillset that will pay dividends personally and professionally for years to come.

To learn more go to:

**www.AmericanGunsmithingInstitute.com**

## Chapter Six

# AGI STUDENT JOURNIES

From David Hill, Owner of DH Gunworks in Evant, TX

David Hill busy gunsmithing.

I'm a graduate of American Gunsmithing Institute's Master Gunsmithing Course. I had my doubts and worries before getting on board with AGI, but none of them turned out to hold any water. Taking this course really has been, and I can tell it will continue to be, life changing.

My journey through this program started about four-and-a-half-months ago when I decided that I wanted to pursue gunsmithing as a profession in my retirement. I'd done all my research from all the online schools to more traditional schools. And for me it really came down to three things. One was the curriculum. I wanted to actually understand how firearms are designed to work so that I was able to fix them. I did not want to be a parts replacer. The other thing was the caliber of the instructors. Then a big one, I hadn't really even thought about it until I made the phone call, was the knowledge of the staff.

There's a lot of places I called and they knew nothing about their curriculum, barely understood it, or they didn't know anything about the industry. If they really want you to be successful, they kind of have to understand all of it. And when I called AGI I was pretty on the fence about it. I didn't know that how this was gonna turn out because it's all video or online. I wondered, "What am I really going to be able to do?" In fact, that was one of my questions that I asked pretty point blank, "What am I going to be able to do when I complete all of this?" And the answer was very quick, without hesitation and to the point, "You're going to be able to fix anything that comes down the road."

I talked to my student advisor at AGI and we had a very real conversation about what I wanted to do, where I wanted to go with this. And we decided that the master gunsmithing course, along with the firearms appraisal course, was going to be my path. It was very easy for me to just say, all right, let's do it. And that's what I did. We had the whole thing done in about 30, 45 minutes. Then as the days went on, I really began to question my decision. Your brain starts running what ifs and all kinds of things.

And I had many arguments with myself about, this probably one of the dumbest things I've done. I just threw away a bunch of money. What can you really learn through videos and online stuff? I remember the night that I had enrolled. My wife and I are sitting at the dinner table and I remember telling her, "I don't know about this. I think I'm just gonna call them and cancel." I was almost sick to my stomach, no joke. It's just a lot of stress. I'm fifty-years-old and the thought of starting over with a new career can be — it's a lot to think about. But this is what I want to do and this is my retirement.

So anyway, I had that mental argument with myself until the courses showed up and basically my mindset was, "They have a hundred percent money back guarantee. I'm going to look at the courses and I'm going to make my mind up." And the first two courses I did was the certified firearms appraiser course and then I started the level one professional gunsmithing course. The first part of that is Introduction to Gunsmithing. I was really blown away with the content. You learn a lot just in the introduction and that pretty much quelled a lot of my doubts about the program being valid. And then it was a matter of, "How am I gonna get business?"

I live out in the middle of nowhere. For me to go grocery shopping it's an hour in any direction. The good news is everything in the AGI course helps you do that. They have a business success package that has all your paperwork, all your Federal Firearms License (FFL) paperwork all your invoices, repair tags, logbooks, and how to approach it, how to be successful. You get all the information you need, from writing ads to how to go out and get work and establish a route. And that's what I did. As I started taking the courses, I took in little projects for that particular part of the course. It wasn't very long that it just got bigger and bigger and bigger and the projects got more and more and more and my confidence got greater and greater and greater.

And you know, here we are four and a half months later. I put in my paperwork and I'm open. It was just time to build the shop and do it for real. All of my doubts were quickly laid to rest.

There's a lot of work out there if you can do it.

Four and a half months ago, I started the master gunsmithing course. I am now an American Gunsmithing Institute Master Gunsmith. What I want you to bear in mind is this all started in my living room on just a little makeshift workbench. And as I went through the curriculum, I just got busier and busier to where I got banished from the house to my tool shed, which was 10ft by 12ft. And it didn't take long before I outgrew that. And honestly, I got far enough along in the program and my confidence was good enough to where it was just time to do the paperwork, pay the fees, and get my FFL so that I could get open. And that's what I did. The shop is 16ft by 32ft. I opened the first week of October and I have been pretty busy. It's just me, but I do a lot of different types of gunsmithing and I just needed to be able to spread out so that I could work on multiple projects at the same time.

Now here's why that's important: I've worked on a lot of guns so far and I'm amazed at what a big difference it makes in my new business to be able to actually make parts. It makes a difference to me and it makes a difference to my customers. Why is that? Because let's say you're fixing a rifle and you don't know how to make a stock or a trigger; you'll have to buy those. And so, you have a rifle that's $250 brand new that you're going to spend another $300 or $400 on and then you've got to probably do something with the barrel. Because I understand design, function, and repair, that makes it very affordable for me to repair or make what's necessary and that savings is passed on to the customer.I don't have to source anything out. There's no parts that I have to buy. He's paying for labor and to be honest, that's good for me as far as profit goes because it's all labor. I don't have any other expenses. That's all it is, is labor. And that goes right to design, function, and repair. I really hope that this helps you out. I hope that it gives you a little bit of confidence to say, "Oh man, this is going to be good." I hope it quells some doubts and answers some questions you might have about the program.

It's a stressful thing to have to do if you're just starting out in life or you're like me and you're changing careers. It's expensive and it's stressful. There were days where I felt this was one of the dumbest decisions I ever made. And I'm going to tell you right now, I'm really glad I made that decision. I opened in October, right around the first of the month. So, I've got October, November, December, and I keep track of expenses and I just use good business sense. I kind of know where I'm going. And so, this is a real number that I'm going to spit out. Right now, I'm looking at between October, by the end of the year, I'll be on track to make from $13,000 to $17,000 in three months.

It's been a lot of work. I open my doors at two o'clock in the afternoon I'm supposed to — the sign says closed at 7:30, but there's not many nights that I'm not down here at 10, 11 o'clock at night. But I just love it. And the work is there. I enjoy the people. They all come in with stories. They all love to talk about guns. They all love to see what you're working on and that gives them confidence in you, so they bring you more work. Other than that, I really do hope this boosts your confidence a little bit and just remember all those guys at AGI are there to there to help you succeed. They're all really good. You just get to be really good friends with them and they help you out a lot. Nobody wants to see you fail. Everybody wants to see you do well. And so good luck and happy gunsmithing.

(To see video of David telling his story and other Successful AGI Professional Gunsmithing Students, go to **www.AgiReviews.com**).

## MORE AGI STUDENT SUCCESS STORIES...

# Glock build becomes a special gift thanks to AGI's Glocksmithing Course

### Contributed by AGI Student Don Harden

I invested in the AGI Certified Glocksmithing Course and after watching Gene Shuey build Glocks, I was hooked. What a marvelous craftsman Mr. Shuey is! I am astounded by the quality of his work!

I had never owned a Glock before. Buy a used one and modify it, or build from parts? I decided a combination would work and that perhaps this gun would be a showcase of what I could do with AGI's and Gene Shuey's guidance. I love the .40 S&W so that would be my caliber choice. I didn't need a carry gun, so why not a target pistol. A model 35 was my pick and I started gathering parts.

I found a used Model 17 frame assembly on GunBroker and bought it. I purchased a .40 caliber Storm Lake barrel from Brownells. The slide came from Lone Wolf. I was influenced by Gene to add the Cominolli safety kit. I reshaped the trigger guard and the trigger area. I took Gene's

AGI Student Don Harden and his daughters Jana and Ashley.

advice and used the trigger that came installed in my used frame.

I installed a Ghost 3.5# connector in the Cominolli trigger housing after I gave it a high polish. I then polished the snot out of the trigger bar and firing pin block plunger! In addition, I polished the contact surfaces on the locking block and the barrel ramp, cam surfaces, and hood and chamber. I then applied one of the Cerakote dark greens to the frame.

For parts in the slide, I purchased a titanium firing pin and installed a lighter weight spring on it. I polished the firing pin block to a mirror finish and installed a lighter spring in it. I double checked the extractor for fit and made some slight changes. The rest of the parts in the slide remained stock.

I had just recently obtained a small mill and was anxious to mill my first slide. I liked what Mr. Shuey did to his slide in the video. I decided I would follow the example in the video but add my own touches. The green Cerakote finish on the frame looked great but how about the slide and barrel? It just all came together in my mind and I knew what I was going to do. I would do the barrel in gold and do the accents on my slide in gold as well. I polished the sides of the slide to a high luster. I had previously sandblasted the top of the slide to eliminate glare.

It just so happened my wife and I had been planning to go see the kids, so I assembled the gun to show it off. I had not decided on sights at this point, so it had none. As planned, my law enforcement daughter Jana joined us for the shooting session. She asked if she could shoot it. I said sure but there aren't any sights on it. She just wanted to see how it felt and try the trigger. From about 10 yards she proceeded to put fifteen rounds into about 2"! She said, "nice gun Dad." During the time I was working on the gun, my daughter Jana had been notified she would be promoted to Captain. I had been thinking about gifting the Glock to Jana in honor of her hard work and promotion and I presented her the Glock. With conditions!! She had to let me fit sights of her choice on it.

I brought the gun home and decided that now, it must be perfect! I put the slide back in my mill and changed the V shaped racing stripes on each side to 1/8" wide grooves. Next, I removed the gold Cerakote from the barrel. I polished the 3 flat sides of the chamber area. I removed the Cerakote I had applied on the slide. I then taped it up again and did the Cerakote again. I added a blue stripe where there had been a gold stripe and repolished the sides of the slide to a bright finish. I then took the slide to a local trophy shop and had Jana's name engraved on it. I returned the gun to Jana three weeks later and she was thrilled.

This is without a doubt the most enjoyable custom pistol I have done to date. The learning experience on this one and the pleasure I got from her appreciation was immeasurable. I guess I will have to build another Glock to use for taking to gun shows. Oh darn!!! Needless to say, the training I have received from AGI is invaluable in learning what and how to do it right!

Enroll in the certified glocksmithingcourse today!

## What Success Looks Like...

**Jed Nadler, AGI pro student, GCA member, gunsmith and business owner**

You guys got good stuff!

After 30 years of working a job I grew tired of, you guys put me into doing something completely different that I really love. And the update? FIRST Gunsmithing now has 3 part time employees. Mike is a smith who is mostly through with the AGI Master course himself. I look for him to buy me out when I finally retire in about 10 years. Dan is a police department armorer who comes in to help a couple of

– Modern
– Technical
– Professional

**GUNSMITH**

A St Louis area full service Gunsmith employing old world craftsmanship with modern technologies.

Store Hours:
Tue-Wed-Thu: 10-6,
Fri-Sat: 10-5,
Closed Sun & Mon

AGI Certified
Master Gunsmith

**FIRST** Gunsmithing, LLC

Firearm Improvement & Repair with Specialized Technologies
932 Meramec Station Rd., Valley Park, MO 63088 • Hwy 141 & I-44
Behind Ruby Tuesday
636-825-6606 • info@FIRSTGunsmithing.com

This is a copy of our ad from the Outdoor Guide magazine in our area. (I'm the one in my trusty AGI apron, which I proudly wear every day.)

times a week. Karen is a temp who takes care of the bookkeeping and inventory. I opened September 1, 2015. On the one year anniversary I took in my 389th gun for repair! I cannot tell you how happy I am with the education I received from AGI. I had very little prior smith experience. All that I learned from the Master Gunsmith course and Gene's additional business advice prepared me very well. Right down to the repair tags, I was able to set up shop and take off. I refer to the course discs on a regular basis to refresh what I've grown hazy on. Plus

I now have a con-
siderable collection
of Armorer Courses
that come in handy
too. And on top of
all of that my Gun-
smithing Club of
America SilverPLUS
membership gives me one more video each month and a forum of
incredible depth of knowledge.

I appreciated every last bit of help the Master Gunsmith Course
brought me. In particular the FFL package helped me over a hurdle
that quite frankly had me worried. The RK Enterprises package
really showed me that you guys really meant to help me get ALL
THE WAY there. And it did. GCA videos and forum help me on
a continuing basis. Between them and the Armorer's Courses I'm
using AGI almost daily. Wait a minute . . . counting the Jack First
and Numrich catalogs, I'm using the course nearly hourly.

### Opening the Gunsmith Shop

I looked at cheaper places, more industrial, more off the beaten
path. The real estate agent really encouraged me to look at this one.
I got a very good deal.

There is a very popular barbeque restaurant that lines people
up every lunch and dinner. I get about 6-10 people through the
door daily saying "I was just down there eating and saw your place.

I didn't know you were here!" The location has really paid off. The landlord and I used the same contractor for the build-out, saving me a lot of money. I did all the painting, all the layout, some of the purchasing and all the clean up, saving me more still. It also didn't hurt that I was here every day making sure every subcontractor got all their questions answered immediately. It has been a remarkable journey. I've been smiling real big for the last 18 months!

## AGI student builds an absolutely stunning custom Mauser hunting rifle with the help of AGI instructional videos - He says you can too!...

" . . . I have been a life long subscriber to Rifle Magazine and have lusted after the beautiful firearms that have been portrayed in their "Custom Corner."

I decided I would attempt to build my own custom rifle. So I began to look around for a resource where I could learn how to do just that. Going to one of the gunsmithing schools

Just gorgeous! Jim proudly displays his handmade custom mauser.

was out of the question considering I wanted to do this as a hobby, not as a profession. I read/heard about your company and decided to take a chance. I ordered the "Building the Custom Mauser." I purchased a Persian 98/29 Mauser rifle and began work.

I wanted to tell you I have watched that series over ten times all the way through. Mr. Shuey is a disciplined instructor, not given to over statement.

71

For the beginner, these videos are so helpful as they walk one through the entire process of building a custom rifle. Then I purchased the Rust /Nitre Bluing. I have just completed all of the metal work (bottom metal, action, bolt and barrel) and I gotta tell you, it is beautiful!

I could never have afforded to purchase a custom rifle of this quality. Yet, with these videos, I have been able to produce beautiful work. This is not a testimony to my own efforts. Rather, this is praise for the ability of these videos to provide instruction in such a way, that a beginner like me can turn out decent work. In the hands of a patient and diligent person, these videos bring the possibility of the custom rifle into the reach of people like me. For that I wish to thank you and your organization for providing me with this service. I got more than I bargained for from your videos!"

Sincerely yours,

*Pastor Jim Pimentel*

To find AGI custom rifle building courses,
go to: **www.AmericanGunsmith.com**

## AGI Student builds Guinness Record Breaking Rifle - accurate to 4300 meters (2.7 miles)!

I wanted to thank all the staff at AGI for everything you have done to ensure your training is the finest available. I am a retired and 70% disabled veteran who spent 22 years in the US Army working in various areas of weapons maintenance. I had a vast amount of experience with current military arms, but I had zero knowledge of civilian firearms. I enrolled through the Vocational Rehabilitation program (VA Ch31) in the Enhanced Master Gunsmith program. In February of 2016 I opened my own shop, Blackstone Valley Precision.

Since that time lessons learned from your instructional videos have been invaluable. I keep the videos close at hand to help refresh my memory on each individual gun I'm working on. In addition to the repair videos, the Business Success Toolkit and additional bonus educational videos on rifle tuning and accuracy enhancement have made a world of difference. They provided the knowledge necessary for me to build a financially viable business in less than one year. But, it doesn't end there.

Most notable for me was when a customer approached me about building him a custom rifle. Unlike previous custom rifle

Nathan Allen

builds, this one had only one purpose, to establish the Guinness world record for long distance shooting. He wanted a rifle capable of hitting a one MOA target, three times consecutively at 4300 meters! He was asking me to build a gun that would accurately shoot 2.7 miles!

Working from scratch, and using all the knowledge provided in the lessons from the Enhanced Master Gunsmith course I was able to build that rifle. But the icing on the cake, is that on June 5th, 2017 Adam Kodra used the rifle I built to establish a recognized world record. On his first practice session, firing from a cold bore, his first round hit the target, he followed up with two more consecutive hits - sealing his place in the record books.

I don't think I can thank AGI enough for providing me with the tools necessary to make that happen, not to mention aiding me in setting up a business that is providing for my family.

Thank you, Nathan Allen, Blackstone Valley Precision, Tomah, WI

Here are the numbers to back up the picture:

The rifle weighs 36 lbs and measures 62 - 1/2" long. The scope is a 35mm tube 7-35X50 Nightforce scope.

I used a Lilja 1:11 twist barrel that I chambered for 416 Barrett (a necked down 50 BMG cartridge). The bullet is a custom made 440 grain solid brass bullet that leaves the muzzle at 3350 FPS and reaches the target at 350 FPS.

*Nathan Allen, BlackStone Valley Precision, Tomah, Wisconsin*

## Chapter Seven

# SETTING UP SHOP

Sean Brooks home based Gunsmithing Shop and workbench.

People that are just getting started in Gunsmithing are often surprised to learn that it doesn't really require a lot of space or expensive equipment to do most types of Gunsmithing work.

In fact, many professional Gunsmiths start out using just four to six feet of extra bench space in their garage, shop or spare bedroom.

To do most types of firearms repairs, you only need basic hand tools such as Screw drivers, pin punches, a few different hammers, some files, pliers, picks, hack saw and a good bench vise. I recommend the Versa Vise or equivalent as it has smooth, parallel jaw sides and pivots easily. It also will clamp parts securely without marring them.

You will need a set of Pin Punches, including; Brass, Nylon and Steel to drive out pins or to move other parts such as sights. It is also a good idea to find a set of long or extended punches. You should have a short "starter" punch to initially start driving a pin out, and then use a longer, close fitting punch to continue to drive the pin through and out the other side of a receiver or part.

To avoid damaging guns and parts, use the appropriate hammer. I use a 2 ounce, a four ounce, and an 8-ounce Ball Peen hammers for most of my gun work. You will also want to have a plastic "No-Mar" hammer, a dead blow hammer and a big rubber mallet.

Almost all gun work will require screwdrivers and it is extremely important that the proper screwdriver be used. Never use a standard screwdriver on a gun. Most screwdrivers have tapered sides of the blade. This allows them to fit a wide variety of screw slot sizes and it also adds strength. But they are NOT Intended to use for working on guns and they should never be used.

The reason is, that a tapered screwdriver will cam against the screw slot as you apply pressure and cause the screwdriver to ride up out of the slot, which will cause it to burr the screw slot and if it slips you could scratch the firearm finish or gouge the wood. Therefore, the sides of the blade should be either hollow ground or be ground with both sides parallel. A hollow ground screwdriver will apply pressure to the bottom of the screw slot, rather than at the top as a tapered screwdriver does. A properly fitting screwdriver will fill the full width of the screw slot, which applies more leverage by moving the forces out to the very edges of the screw head.

Using a poorly fitting screwdriver leaves unprofessional looking damage that might even require you to refinish the firearms at your expense. So, get the right screwdrivers. The American Gunsmithing Institute teaches you how to properly grind your screw drivers to fit any screw. However, there are also "Gunsmithing Screw Drivers" that have parallel blades and magnetic multi-tip driver sets that are "hollow ground" and designed for Gunsmithing use.

A screwdriver must fit exactly in the slot of the screw, both in length and width. When you twist the screwdriver, the blade transfers the force to both sides of the screw slot in the direction you want the screw to go. Using the wrong or poorly fitting

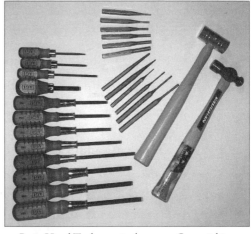

Basic Hand Tools required to start Gunsmithing

screwdriver on a tight screw will result in the screw slot becoming damaged. A badly damaged screw may require drilling to get out, so avoid creating the situation in the first place by using properly fitting screwdrivers. There are numerous multi-tip screwdriver sets available from companies such as Lyman, Wheeler Engineering, Brownells and others that have numerous blade sizes so that you can find a tip that fits the screw slot properly.

Some additional hand tools that you will want for working on firearms include:

- An Allen Wrench Set for socket head screws.

- Steel Dental and Nylon Picks are used to scrap parts clean and to hook a spring and pull it out of a hole among other uses.

- An Exacto-knife or other precision hand held cutting tools enables you to cut tape to fit, or remove small amounts of wood.

- You will use a digital caliper almost constantly to measure parts and a one-inch micrometer. You will also use a tape measure and a six-inch metal machinist ruler.

- Wrenches and Socket Set to remove stock bolts.

- A Screw Pitch Gauge, these are used to tell you the thread pitch of an existing screw.

- A Tap and Die Set for when you are drilling and tapping a hole to fit a specific screw. For example, when mounting a sight or scope on a firearm that isn't pre-drilled and tapped at the factory.

- A Bench block which is a plastic or nylon block with holes in it. They are used to support parts during certain operations. For example, if you are driving a pin out of a hammer, you can put it on the bench block and then you can drive the pin out of the part and into the hole while the part is fully supported.

- A long gun vise, that will hold rifles/shotguns is handy to have. They hold a full-size gun in the horizonal position so that you can mount a scope, or clean it without damaging it.

- An LED Flashlight and those with flexible heads are very handy for seeing into actions and looking for dropped parts.

You will also need a set of wood and metal files. Files come in various cut types, such as mill files, double cut files, and rough "Bastard" files. They also come in different sizes. Common sizes for Gunsmithing purposes are 6", 8" and 10" long files, although you will use others. Another file type is "jewelers files" which fit into small places and are generally finer in finish. These generally come in sets. Files also come in various shapes, such as flat, round, half-round, and others. A good mix will be handy to have and I have found that you can buy high quality files such as the Nicholson brand in pre-assembled sets to cover most of your needs. From time to time you will need a specialty file, for cutting a dovetail slot for a sight, or checkering metal. These are available from Gunsmithing tool suppliers.

To keep your files sharp and cutting smoothly, you will need to remove the metal filings stuck in the "teeth", to do so you need what is called a "card", it is a brush intended to remove the filings from the teeth. You will want to do that from time to time as you are filing as the metal builds up in the teeth. Some files come with handles, but most do not. You want to put a handle on the files to protect your hands. Store files carefully so that they stay sharp and cut cleanly.

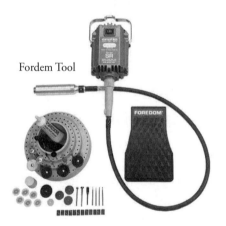

Fordem Tool

For fine polishing of parts, such as "Sears" or Trigger Connectors, you need to have a set of "stones." Both natural and man-made stones are available in various grades, such as fine, medium and coarse. To start with get a set of aluminum-oxide stones, one in a rectangular or square shape, and the other a triangular stone. Get both in fine or extra-fine grade to start.

It is also important to have the one power tool that I consider mandatory for professional Gunsmithing work, and that is a Foredom Tool, which is an electric powered hand-chuck with a flexible shaft and a foot-controlled speed pedal. This is the one power tool that you will use more than any other in your general Gunsmithing work. With it you can; drill, grind, polish, cut, and do many other tasks with a great deal of control. The USA made unit by Blackstone Industries is what we recommend and the brand name is Foredom. They cost less than $500 and yet will handle most of the required tasks in a general repair gunshop.

In order of importance I would also add the following power tools; Belt sander, (either a 1" to 2 " belt sander with a disc sander on the side or a 2" quick change belt sander), A bench top or free standing drill press, a bench grinder, and a small bench top lathe.

Then a gas welding set-up with torches and tanks, a TIG welding machine, and finally when you need them; a full-size lathe (for barrel work), and finally a milling machine. You might also like to have a table saw for wood work (cutting stocks for recoil pads) and a metal cutting Band Saw.

You don't need to invest in all of this at once. In fact, unless you are doing barreling work and are milling slides or creating tooling, you really don't need a full-size lathe or milling machine at all. A bench lathe will enable you to re-tip firing pins, polish parts and screws, turn small parts, do pistol barrel set-backs and more.

In time you can acquire everything you need by buying the tools you need for the specific job each time you start a new project and soon, you will have a pretty well outfitted shop.

Ideally, any work area should be well lighted. Now you can buy LED lights that will last for years. You want to get your lighting as even as possible so hang the lights above your work area and also have additional lights that you can focus onto your work area. Remember to mount the lights high enough so that you don't hit them with the barrel of a rifle or shotgun when you are moving them around.

The work bench should be the right height for working while standing up. That means it needs to be higher than most tables or desks. A good rule of thumb for measuring is to stand comfortably on the surface that you will be using (don't forget to include a soft pad for standing comfort), then while standing hold your hands out with your palms facing downward and your elbows bent at a comfortable angle of approximately 90 degrees. The bench height should be just a bit less than that height.

Have someone help you measure for that, because it will be about the right height for working on guns. For most people this is going to work out to be about 36 to 42 inches high. If it is too low you will hurt your back bending over too much. If it is too high it will feel awkward.

You want to be able to reach your tools mounted on the wall at the back of the bench so depending on your length of your arm, it can be around 24 to 32 inches deep. Again, you don't want it too deep as you will be reaching a lot for tools that are mounted on the wall. The top should extend over the cabinets at least 6 to 8 inches or more so that you can comfortably stand or sit with your knees under the bench top. You are also probably going to use an adjustable stool to sit on.

The bench should be really thick and solid. You will need to mount one or two vises to the bench top. So, keep that in mind when you are laying out your workbench design. Often you want to have the bench top built of several layers of wood. This creates a "deadening effect" where everything doesn't bounce when you pound on it. This is one area not to cut corners. The bench only needs to be 6 to 8 feet long. However, I have worked in gunshops where the benches went all around the walls, with cabinets underneath them. This is convenient when you have multiple projects that you are working on and you want to spread out.

I like to cover the bench in a thin commercial grade carpet that is basically smooth. Then I use carpet sample size pieces of a medium plush (1/4" to 3/8") to lay the guns on that I am actually working on. This keeps them from getting scratched, catches pins and screws that I take out, and when dirty are easier to clean or get rid of, enabling me to keep the base carpet relatively clean.

Closed cabinets and a smooth face under the front of the bench are highly desirable. Because if you have open shelves with lots of junk stacked there, it will be easy to lose parts rather than have them drop straight to the floor. (that tip alone will save you hours of doing the "Gunsmith crawl" looking for dropped parts!)

Use pegboard at the back of the bench top on the wall to hang your tools and have them easily accessible. There are a variety of hangers available for screwdrivers, punches, files, hammers, etc.

You will be using your vise for some aspect on almost every job. Buy a good steel one. Again, the Versa Vise brand or equal is recommended. Make sure you can swivel it around freely 360 degrees and that it has flat, four to six inch wide, smooth, parallel jaws. You can make or buy padded vise jaws that go over the metal ones and further help prevent damaging parts or enable you to hold certain parts better. You will be using this vise a lot, so make sure that it is securely mounted.

I also like to have a second vise, a large one that is more of a traditional shop vise for use in bending parts or pounding on. The vises should be mounted solidly on your bench and you may need to reinforce them from underneath. Locate the vises on corners of the bench so it's not in the way, but is easy to access when you do need it.

Versa Vise

It is very handy to have compressed air to blow off parts. To get started, you can use "canned air" which is just compressed air in a can with a spray nozzle. But using those can get expensive after a while, so soon you will want a small portable size air compressor. If you have the shop space, get a bigger one, with enough volume for spraying and sandblasting applications, 20 to 30 gallons size is good. Add an in-line filter to make sure the air is clean and free of water.

Other handy shop tools for Gunsmithing (many that you might already have) include; a handheld cordless battery powered drill, a full set of drill bits, (including inch and number drills), a handsaw, pliers, cutters and tweezers. With the appropriate blade, a table saw is also useful for other gunsmithing related jobs dealing with wood or plastic.

Always remember to wear eye protection when working on guns. Safety glasses are mandatory, as you never know when a spring will fly out as you disassemble an unfamiliar firearm, or when a piece of debris might hit you in the eye when you are cutting or grinding a part.

Ultra Sonic Cleaner

You, of course, will also be using cleaning equipment, such as brushes, cleaning rods and a small parts cleaning tank. If you are doing a large volume of cleaning jobs, I highly recommend an Infante ultrasonic cleaner. There are several available that are intended to be used to clean firearm parts.

Beyond these items, you will want to acquire tools, fixtures and other items on an "as needed" basis. I know a lot of people enjoy buying and owning a lot of tools, but try and restrain yourself so that you can spend your money buying the best when you need them.

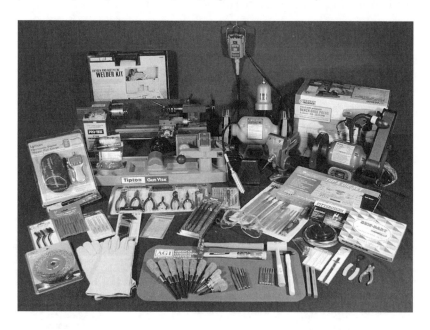

Everything you need to do complete gunsmithing repairs and basic customizing. Our Master Gunsmith Instructors were all consulted and their recommendations are included in this package.

## Recommended Tool List

7" x 12" Bench Top Lathe

6" Wire Wheel

Belt Sander with Disk Sander

Bench Grinder and Wire Brush

Bench Top Drill Press

Gunsmith Bench Vise – a solid steel vise with wide parallel jaws

Foredom Hand Grinder with cutters and bits, including Flex Shaft, Handle and Variable Speed Foot Control.

Oxy-Acetylene Torch, Tip and Regulator Kit (tanks not included)

AGI Hand Tool Set: Complete Set of Gunsmithing Screw Drivers Brass Punch Set, Steel Pin Punch Set, 4-ounce Ball Peen Hammer

9-ounce Brass Hammer

Gun Kote Airbrush Metal Finishing Kit – refinish firearms with multi-color state of the art finishes.

2-ounce Ball Peen Hammer

Plastic Mallet

6 inch Diagonal Cutter

Dental Pick Set

Professional File Set & Rasp Set

Needle File Set

Safety Glasses

Thread Gauge

Gunsmith Bench Block

Digital Calipers

Laser Boresighting System (for collimating scopes)

Electronic Trigger Pull Gage

Rifle Holding Cleaning Fixture and Cradle

6" x ½" Norton Trigger and Sear Stones (fine and medium)

Screw Gizzie (for grinding screws to fit)

Gunsmith Parallel Jaw Pliers

Mauser Bolt Extractor Pliers

Holland Scope Mounting Fixture

Miles Gilbert Recoil Pad Installation Kit

Screw Checker (size and thread pitch)

33 Piece Precision Screwdriver Set

Cleaning Rods and Brushes

Magnetic Dish (to prevent losing parts)

Mini Pick & Hook Set

Tap & Die Set

Tweezer Set

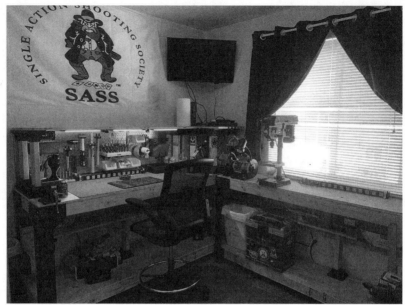

A well-organized, home based Gunsmithing workbench. Note that everything is within easy reach. – Photo courtesy of AGI Professional Gunsmithing Student Sean Brooks.

Note: To see a tour of an actual gunsmithing gunshop go to: **www.gunsmithingcourse.com.**

# COMMON GUNSMITHING BUSINESS RELATED Q&A'S

I often host webinars where I answer peoples questions about becoming a professional gunsmith. What follows are many of the common questions I have received along with my answers. For continuity of thought, I have grouped them into chapters covering the following subjects:

*NOTE: I am not an Attorney. What follows is NOT legal advice. These answers are just my opinions based on my personal experiences. Your experience or outcomes may be different. For legal advice consult an attorney. For questions about getting a Federal Firearms License, manufacturing firearms, transferring firearms, required record keeping, applying for a Federal Firearms License and other federal regulatory and legal issues related to firearms, contact the Bureau of Alcohol, Tobacco, Firearms and Explosives (BATFE). www.ATF.gov*

*NOTE: Individual States have firearms laws that may affect your operating a firearms or Gunsmithing business. Check all state and local laws. Or contact a firearms attorney to receive specific advice.*

## Chapter Eight

# QUESTIONS ABOUT FEDERAL FIREARMS LICENSES (FFL)

### Do I need a Federal Firearms License to be a Gunsmith?

If you're charging for Gunsmithing work or keeping other people's firearms overnight, then Yes, you do need a Federal Firearms License (FFL). It is not hard to get one in most cases and we provide AGI Students with a step-by-step process to successfully get their FFL on their first attempt. (For official information how to get your FFL, go to www.ATF.gov for details)

## Do you already have to be a Gunsmith to get an FFL? Should a person apply for their license before starting or after completing a gunsmithing course?

It is not required that you already be a Gunsmith to get an FFL. You can go through the entire Gunsmithing course if you want without an FFL, but it'll be more difficult for you in that you can't buy and sell guns at wholesale, you can't bring in guns from people that are paying you and keep them overnight, etc. But you don't have to be a gunsmith to get an FFL.

Anybody can apply for an FFL as long as you're not a prohibited person, meaning that you're NOT a felon or someone that has a disqualifying misdemeanor, restraining order, or something that would stop you from being able to buy or possess a firearm. If you can buy a firearm, then you should be able to get an FFL. The only other issue that might arise is the location from which you are planning on operating your business must be within local zoning requirements, if there are any. In many areas you can operate a business out of your home. And if you can operate any business legally out of your home, you can also generally operate a Gunsmithing business out of your home.

## How complicated of a process is getting your FFL?

It is really as simple as properly filling out the application form and submitting it with the appropriate fees, which are currently only $200 for a three-year license. If you submit a properly filled out application and are not a "Prohibited Person", it's really pretty straight forward and it only takes approximately 90 days from the time you submit your application to receive your FFL.

The system we provide our students walks you through the application it step-by-step. We've even created a video webinar for our students with our FFL Application expert who has personally helped thousands of people get their FFL.

## What category of FFL do most gunsmiths pursue?

Generally, you would select one of two primary categories of FFLs as a Gunsmith. The majority of General Repair and Customizing Gunsmiths should get a type one license, also known as a "01" license. It allows you to buy and sell guns just like a regular firearms dealer but it's also the classification that most Gunsmithing is performed under. There isn't a separate license just for Gunsmithing. Currently Gunsmiths can "manufacture" up to 49 firearms annually under this type of license without having to pay the Excise Tax that regular manufacturers have to pay on all firearms that they produce.

The second type license you might want to consider is the type seven license, also known as a "07," which a manufacturer's license. This license enables you to manufacture standard firearms, including semi-automatic firearms. In addition to licensing fees, you will have to pay an Excise Tax on the firearms you manufacture and sell.

This is the type of license that our company has. We also have an SOT, Special Occupational Taxpayers stamp. So, they call that a "Class 2 manufacturer." Under that combination of the 07 manufacturers license and the "Tax Stamp" we can manufacture NFA (National Firearms Act) weapons, and such as machineguns, suppressors, etc.

If you want to be a "Class 3 dealer", and just buy and sell machine guns, short barrel firearms, and suppressors, you pay the SOT "Tax Stamp" annually on top of your 01 license.

With a manufacturer type 07 license, you can still buy, and sell firearms the same way as a 01 regular dealer would.

So, my recommendation is that a 01 license is probably best and most common for General Gunsmithing, but you should apply for an 07 manufacturer's license if you're going to be in the business of building firearms.

Note: For a definition of "manufacturing" check with Bureau of Alcohol Tobacco Firearms and Explosives (BATFE).

## Why would you recommend an FFL type 01 instead of an 07?

Well, I don't recommend one versus the other. It's really depends on what you want to do. So, if you want to be a manufacturer, then you need to get an 07 license. If you want to manufacture automatic weapons, you need to have an 07 license plus an SOT, a special occupational taxpayer stamp. And you're going to have to register with State Department when you manufacture automatic weapons and suppressors. If you just want to manufacturer standard firearms, then just an 07 license is perfect.

But if you're going to build hunting rifles? No problem. A regular 01 license will do just fine. If you are offering general Gunsmithing and repairing and fixing guns, or buying and selling guns, an 01 license is what you will want to apply for.

There is also a little more paperwork involved with an 07 manufacturers license. There's annual production reporting. There could be tax involved. If you produce firearms and you sell the firearms you produce, there's an excise tax on those firearms that you have to report and pay.

The Excise Tax is approximately 11% of what you sell the product for. There are pros and cons really, depending on what you want to do. I would say generally, it's a little bit easier to get a 01 license just anywhere, versus if you're getting a manufacturing license, and you're in a 10 by 10 room, they're going to be kind of asking, "Well, how are you going to do this manufacturing?"

So tell them the truth. It could be: "Right now, I'm in the prototyping stage and I'm having some stuff subcontracted, but I'm doing the final work on making the receiver here, and so I need a 07 for proper licensing and record keeping." Or whatever is your actual situation. But as far as what license you apply for, it really depends on what you want to accomplish in your business and what is required to stay within the law.

Isn't the Bureau of Alcohol Tobacco Firearms and Explosives (BATFE) really hard to deal with!?

In my experience, if you are not a criminal and aren't doing anything illegal, you won't have a problem. In fact, most of the ATF agents that I have dealt with are really good guys and gals. Just like anyone else, if you approach them honestly and are straight forward, they are generally going to try and help you do things right. I'm hearing from a lot of our students that they're not having any problems getting their licenses, especially if they approach it professionally. Follow our FFL application process that we provide you with our courses, but also be an upstanding person yourself. Act professional, look professional, be organized and you're going to get respect, and not have any problems.

## Do you think it will become more difficult to get an FFL?

Frankly I don't know. I wouldn't bet against it because politicians always have a new rule that they just love to put on us. But I will tell you, just go ahead and get one now. If you're not in the game, get in. Get an FFL for crying out loud. It's not that hard and the cost for the license is only $200 for three years. Once you have a license it will be easier to keep it if the rules ever change.

I've had a license for, over 40 years. It's not that big of deal to get and it enables you to purchase o firearms, ammunition and accessories at wholesale! It will also allow you to, as a gunsmith, with the right certifications, some manufacturers will give you access to parts that are restricted. So, yeah. Big advantage. I'd do it and I'd do it now because if you're in the game you're going to be a whole lot better off than if you're not in the game if anything changes.

## Should I use my home address for the FFL?

Well, that depends. It depends upon where you want to operate from. In most areas of the country you can still get a business license doing services from your home. If that's your situation, and you want to work from your home, then your FFL must be at your home. If you want to be working from a commercial location, then that's where your FFL must be.

Another option is that you could share a shop with another FFL dealer. They have their regular dealer business, and you're just doing the gunsmithing. You can either work under their license, or you can have your own FFL license at that same location.

## Can you add a business name later to the FFL?

You can change and amend your FFL anytime you need to. However, you may find yourself in a position where you can't continue to operate until you get that updated FFL. Changing the business name isn't something you want to do lightly, and particularly if ownership or responsible party changes, you have to notify ATF of that. You would have to notify ATF of any name change, or any address change. However, the regulations about those situations are very straightforward. You can go on ATFs website or look in the regulation books and get all the details there.

## Can you have more than one FFL?

The answer is yes. You can have more than one location, and each Location needs its own FFL. Our corporation has more than one FFL location. Why? Because we have locations where we are operating firearms facilities in more than one state filming videos, receiving firearms, doing Gunsmithing work and so on. We do everything legally, so we have an FFL in each of those locations. Most Gunsmiths would only want one FFL.

## My (Big Liberal City) doesn't allow an FFL dealer to get a license. Is there any way around that?

Well, I will say this. There's always a way around everything if you're willing to jump through the hoops. Sometimes you've got to be a little creative. Sometimes you've got to make the right contacts or create the right contractual relationships. I'm sure that there probably is a way, even in (Big Liberal City). Maybe not at a residence, maybe it has to be at a commercial location, but if you want this bad enough, you will find a way. Also, I don't know how far away you are from the next city, county or whatever. But you may be able to more easily get a license in that different city and just drive a bit to work.

People commute for jobs all the time. Maybe it's worth commuting if it's easier for you to get the license that you want. I would also say that it is a business, and you'll have to factor those costs into the overall picture. However much of the time a commercial address is not that expensive to operate from because most gunsmithing shops can work fine in a small 10-foot by 10-foot room. You could find some space to lease or subcontract, those are all appropriate, as long as you can get a local license. You will also want to make sure that you are able to safely secure and store the firearms and your records.

## As a Gunsmith should I incorporate or create an LLC?

The reason to have an LLC or a S corporation, C corporation, or other corporate type of business structure, is primarily to provide protection and a separation of assets of your business from your personal assets. By setting up an LLC or an S corporation, you have now all the business assets AND liabilities within that corporation.

Now when I was starting off, I didn't set up a corporation because I didn't have a lot of personal assets. But later as I got more successful, I incorporated the business to protect myself.

It's not very expensive to put together an LLC or an S corporation. And you can find places online where you can get it done very inexpensively, or you can engage an attorney.

Now, I'm not an attorney and I am NOT providing legal advice. I'm just offering my personal experience, observations, and opinions. I'm not offering any legal advice. But I've had an FFL, for 40 plus years and I've gone through several different versions of it. As an 01, a regular dealer to being an 07 manufacturer, to being an 07 with an SOT special occupational taxpayer stamp, which allows me to work on and build NFA weapons. I've got a pretty broad experience in this.

## Do you give up any rights when you get your FFL?

No. There's this idea that when you get an FFL, that ATF can come into your house or place of business 24 hours a day. That's just not true. A Federal Firearms License is just that. A license to do business. When you fill out your application, and we teach about this, you fill in the times that you are normally planning on operating your business. Such as 9 am to 3pm on Saturdays. Then that is the only time that they can come into your business to do an inspection.

Unless, of course, you're doing something illegal. I mean, if you're doing something illegal, FFL or no FFL, they can come in and arrest you for that. Don't do anything illegal.

But you are not giving up any rights as a federal firearms licensee.

## Do I have to have an FFL to take the AGI Gunsmithing course?

No, you don't have to have an FFL to enroll in a Gunsmithing Course. It's just that the sooner you get your federal firearms license, you will be able to buy in guns, to bring in work, to get your Gunsmithing business rolling.

## I'm going to move in a year, so would it be better to wait until I move to get my federal firearms license?

It depends. It's not that difficult to change a license location. The biggest thing I would say is right now, it's very, very easy to get your license. If you get your license now, and it's a little more difficult in a year or two, you'll already have it. And all you need to do is put in your address change, and there's a form for that available on the BATFE website. www.ATF.gov

## Do you have to have a CCP (Concealed Carry Permit) to get the course and an FFL?

No, as long as you are not a prohibited person and you're over the age of 18. Or, if you're under 18 (we've had people as young as 13 be enrolled in the Professional Gunsmithing course), you need to have a guardian or parental letter. If you're over 18, our only requirements are that you are not a felon or a not a prohibited person. Because those people cannot, in most cases, get a federal firearms license and therefore can't become Gunsmiths.

## Who do I contact to find out if my city or county will allow me to open up a gunsmithing shop?

Now it varies a little bit in each county and city, and state to state, but generally it's going to be whoever controls the issuing of business licenses.

In some rural counties you don't even need a business license. And if none is required, then you're not restricted at all. If you are in an area that requires a business license, and most do, then you need to go about it systematically.

And one of the first things you need to ask, is you need to ask, "Is it OK for me to operate a business, a service business, out of my home?" In this first stage, you don't even need to tell them yet what type of business it is. There's a process to this. We strongly recommend that you follow our FFL Application process step-by-step, and we provide that information to each student when they enroll in the American Gunsmithing Institute, Professional Gunsmithing Course.

## Do you recommend applying for the FFL as soon as we enroll and receive the course material?

Yes, I do. Because the sooner you have your FFL, the sooner you can start taking in firearm to work on and keep them in inventory. Even if you're not totally ready to work on something, you can log them in to your record book and have them in your inventory for as long as it takes for you to work on them. It also allows you to start buying gun, ammo and parts wholesale, as well as being able to sell them to your customers.

*PLEASE NOTE: I am not an Attorney. These answers are just my opinions based on my personal experiences. Your experience or outcomes may be different. For Legal Advice consult an Attorney. For questions about getting a Federal Firearms License, manufacturing firearms, transferring firearms, required record keeping, applying for a Federal Firearms License and other federal regulatory and legal issues related to firearms, Contact the Bureau of Alcohol, Tobacco, Firearms and Explosives (BATFE). www.ATF.gov*

*NOTE: Individual States have firearm laws that may affect your operating a firearms or Gunsmithing business. Check all State and local laws. Or contact a firearms attorney to receive specific advice.*

## Chapter Nine

# QUESTIONS ABOUT STARTING YOUR GUNSMITHING BUSINESS

## My wife is hesitant about starting our own business. Can you talk about the benefits and the risks?

I would encourage you both to look into the many benefits of having a small business in America. It is one of the last, really great opportunities for the average family. Especially a part-time or retirement business that adds extra income to your overall budget that can be used to pay bills or invest in the future.

There are many hidden benefits of owning a business. Especially with a home-based type business, where you can make a good income without a lot of capital expense or overhead. Plus in many cases you can legally deduct, as business expenses, items you're probably paying for already.

Possible business deductions might include; your sample guns that are used for demonstration purposes, Gunsmithing tools, internet, phone, truck or car, business travel, Gun Club Memberships, ammo, attendance at Trade Shows and Gun Shows. Possibly some hunting expenses as they relate to your business and customers. The potential list for all the different things you may be able to legally deduct goes on and on. Now let me say; *Everybody's situation is different and I'm not a CPA or an attorney. I am not giving legal advice. Check with your Tax Advisor. But I want you to know that there are definitely opportunities to change your financial situation for the better.*

When it comes to money, are you aware, that there are "pre-tax dollars" and "post-tax dollars"? Most people who get a paycheck are having to buy these same things we just listed with post-tax dollars. Taxes have already been taken out of their pay check. So if you got paid $100 and you are at a 30% tax level you really only have $70 or the equivalent of only $0.70 cents on the dollar that you get to decide where to spend it. Uncle Sam already took 30% from you. For many people, when you add in all of the State and Local taxes, you might be paying as much as 40 to 50% in taxes.

But if you spend that same dollar <u>before taxes inside a business</u> *and* if it is legally deductible as an expense, you're getting to control 100 percent of that dollar. It even extends to things like providing health care for yourself through your business. So owning a business and paying legally deductible expenses through it can be a huge advantage that others just don't have.

Let me share with you a big secret about successful businesses in America. Here's what is it; The majority of millionaires in the USA today are small business owners. They have been often referred to as "The Millionaire Next Door" and entire books have been written about them. They got that way by owning a money making small business and taking advantage of the tax benefits.

As a part time business, a full-time business, or as a retirement income, a Gunsmithing business is hard to beat. Because it's very low overhead, and you don't have a big capital investment like you do if you were to purchase a franchise or many other businesses. For example a "name brand" sandwich shop franchise requires a minimum investment of $125,000 to a quarter million dollars and that's just to buy the franchise. That doesn't include renting the space, outfitting everything, employees and more.

There isn't a franchise I can think of that is as inexpensive as investing in training yourself to be a Certified Professional Gunsmith. You probably even own many of the tools you need to get started.

There is risk to everything in life, but in my view, **the biggest risk is doing nothing** and having opportunities in life pass you by. Many times you don't get a second chance. So get started now!

## Can you suggest a way to make some easy, quick income while I am studying the Gunsmithing course?

One of the fastest ways you can make money and get experience working on a lot of firearms is to offer professional cleaning and maintenance services.

There are an estimated 385 million privately owned firearms in the USA. With tens of millions of guns added every year. If even 10% of those guns need professional cleaning, repair or customizing, that's means there are over 38 million firearms that need work now. That is Huge. And as you're probably aware, finding a good gunsmith is pretty tough to do. We're training hundreds of new Gunsmiths every year, but the market keeps growing even faster. So there's always a need for more gunsmiths.

To get our new Gunsmiths started, and help them make money even while they are just starting their studies, AGI created a system for marketing and selling professional gun cleaning services. You can learn all about it and watch a short video showing how the system works at **www.ProGunCleaningSystem.com**

## If Gunsmithing from place of residence do you advise to creating an LLC?  Should one carry insurance just in case something goes bad?

I'm an advocate for separating your personal assets from your business assets. It's not hard to do. You can create a 'C' Corporation, an 'S' Corporation, or a Limited Liability Company (LLC). I go into detail about this the business success course section that comes with the AGI Master Gunsmithing Course. But ultimately it depends upon your personal situation. If you don't have a lot of personal assets, it's probably less of an issue. Now I want you to know that Gunsmiths very rarely get sued. Especially if you have the proper training and follow a proven process. In fact, I have actually never heard of one of our American Gunsmithing Institute graduates getting sued.

Now, that doesn't mean you should go without business insurance. There are a number of companies that do offer insurance for Gunsmiths. We provide you a list of them when you enroll in the Professional Gunsmithing course. Gunsmithing insurance is not expensive, and varies depending on how big your business is and where it is located.

I think it is a good idea for many people to separate their business assets from their personal assets by creating an inexpensive corporate structure.  You don't necessarily have to do it right away, though. I didn't. I operated as sole proprietor for a lot of years and then I change my business to an 'S' Corporation when I started to develop assets and wanted to better protect myself. But in my forty plus years of having an FFL, building guns, and Gunsmithing, I have never been sued.

The main thing is to know exactly how to do the work properly and to always check your work for safe operation of the firearm. By understanding Design, Function and Repair (D,F,&R) you will know exactly what you're doing when you repair or alter a firearm. What is dangerous is when people without proper training are installing parts or changing features on firearms. They think they know what they are doing but they're not quite 100% sure. And *THAT* is extremely scary to me, because those people could create an unsafe condition resulting in someone getting seriously hurt. I think you will agree, we never want to risk doing that. So get the proper Design, Function and Repair training and you will avoid making mistakes.

## As someone who does not have a great deal of experience with gun repair, at what point during my Gunsmithing studies would I start attempting hands-on applications of the course material?

You can actually start applying what you're learning almost immediately. Particularly if you're working on your own guns initially. The absolutely worst thing that could happen is that maybe you break something. While that might sound scary to you now,

QUESTIONS ABOUT STARTING YOUR GUNSMITHING BUSINESS

as you study the AGI Gunsmithing Course, pretty soon you will realize, "Wow, I can fix this."

Something the American Gunsmithing Institute exclusively offers, is that if you are working on either your or a customer's gun and you get in over your head, we have gunsmiths that will fix it for you. You'll pay for the repair, but it'll be reasonable and they'll tell you what they did to fix it. However when you go through the Design, Function and Repair training and understand what you're doing, very quickly you're not going to need that support.

It is actually pretty seldom that an AGI student ever needs to send in a gun for help with a repair, but it's good to know the service is there to bail you out if you need it. Just knowing *that* gives our students more confidence to try new challenges. AGI has your back!

So start working on some of your own guns right as soon as you have started studying the Gunsmithing Course. Another way to get some good experience is to buy some kit guns like, for example a 1911 pistol frame and all the parts, essentially a "build it yourself kit".

As you go through the Professional Gunsmithing course and you're learning to build and fitting the parts properly, you will understand WHY you need to do it a certain way. Not just throwing them together and hoping it goes "bang." Because if for example you don't have your lockup fitted right, you're going shoot 100 rounds and it's going to start tear up the locking lugs in the slide and damage other parts. So you certainly need to understand what you're doing. We also recommend that you buy some broken and used guns to practice on as well. You might find some real deals and be able to make a profit by fixing and reselling them.

So there are a lot of great ways you can find guns to work on. There's also friends and family. I do recommend you get an FFL before you are keeping guns overnight that belong to other people or if you're charging money for your work. At that point you are required to have an Federal Firearms License (FFL). In most cases you can easily get your FFL. Then when a firearm is brought in for repair or customizing, you simply write it into your Gunsmith logbook and when you return the firearm you just log it out.

## How do I find Customers?

Once you receive your Gunsmithing Certificate, you should start advertising at Local Shooting Ranges, at Gun Stores, Gun Clubs, and in your local papers offering Firearms Cleaning and Maintenance. This will get you started. And once the word is out that you are Gunsmithing, to a large degree, your customers will find you.

In AGI's Master Gunsmithing Course, there is a complete course on how to market your business.

## How do I grow my business?

What I encourage everyone to do is to build a customer mailing list so that you literally can control your income by communicating with your customer base. When you have both a emailing list and an actual mailing list, you can consistently run some specials, run some add-ons, offer specific customizing promotions, like "Glock Trigger Jobs" one month and "S&W Revolver Trigger Jobs "the next. Then maybe "Rifle bedding, Choke Installation, Scope Mounting, etc., etc." You get the idea. By rotating through specific offers, you can set up to do multiple customers guns and be more efficient.

The main point is that with a successful business, you don't just open the door and wait for someone to walk in. You want to have a steady flow of work so you can even know what your next month's level of income looks like. In fact, most gunsmiths are backed up with months of interesting work.

## How do I get over being afraid to get started?

When you take a positive first step, such as enrolling in a Gunsmithing Course, the fear falls away. Because; *Action eliminates fear.*

Here's the number-one thing I find with people that are successful, they just don't let anything stop them. They decide they want to do something and if they hit a wall one way, they either go through the wall, under the wall, or over the wall, or go 90 degrees and figure a way around the wall. You got to just keep going and decide what you want and then go for it. AGI can provide you the training. We have for thousands of people. You just need to provide the drive and the desire.

## What do you think will happen as far as gun control? Will there be a need for any new gunsmiths?

For over 40 years people have been concerned and afraid of the government stepping on their firearm rights, and yet the need for gunsmiths is greater now than it ever has been. And I believe it will continue to be for several reasons. "Gun Control" really isn't popular with the majority of people in the United States. In spite of that, Extreme Liberals have tried again and again, and again to take our firearms from us, but it hasn't happened yet and I don't think it will. We have the protections granted us by the Second Amendment, and thankfully, we've got a Supreme Court that, at the moment, is going to defend that right.

Even in countries where it is very difficult to own firearms, gunsmiths make a good living because the firearms that people have, they can't easily replace by just going buy another one. So they are more than willing to pay to maintain and repair them.

There are somewhere around 385 million firearms in the United States. Yearly productions reports show that additional millions of firearms are added to the overall inventory each year. People love their guns. They're not going to give them up. And they are also going to want to get them repaired, maintained, and customized. So, yes there's still an excellent opportunity for properly trained Gunsmiths.

What I would encourage you to do is enroll in a professional Gunsmithing Course and apply for your Federal Firearms License (FFL), because once you are in the business you've got more protection and it's easier to stay in business with access to firearms, parts and ammo, rather than trying to get a license if they add more rules later.

## What's the market price to charge for doing a cleaning and maintenance job on a handgun?

It really depends on your area. But when using the AGI Ultra-Sonic Gun Cleaning System and the process we teach to do fast professional cleanings with the goal of creating new and repeat customers, we often recommend charging somewhere in the $39 to $49 range for each cleaning.

The goal of bringing the guns in for the initial cleaning should be just the first step in providing a series of profitable services such as repair, restoration and customizing jobs. Using our UltraSonic Cleaning system and following our process, you could easily clean four handguns an hour, which means if you are charging just $39.95 each, you would be basically making $160 an hour. (4 guns x $40 = $160) I'm not saying you're going to make that hour after hour, but you can certainly have some very well paid hours.

In addition to that, when you sit down with the customer, there will be some obvious and legitimate repairs or upsells that they should want or need that they are willing to pay extra for. So each cleaning job generates a lot more income if you approach it right.

The American Gunsmithing Institute has also created an exclusive "Gunsmithing job rate book" manual. We include that with our Master Gunsmithing Course and it will help you determine what you should charge for a wide variety of Gunsmithing jobs.

## What does the average Gunsmiths charge per hour?

It really varies widely around the country as the cost of living varies so much. What I usually suggest is that you compare your hourly rates to that of a local automotive shop. So if you're trying to set a price of what you should charge, find out what an automotive shops in your areas charge. In Northern California they currently charge about $150 an hour.

Because Gunsmithing shops typically don't have anywhere near the overhead and tool expense that an automotive shop does, meaning; lift racks, alignment machines and all of the electronic diagnostic equipment required. You can generally start out charging a lower rate. Probably around half. So in this case $75 an hour.

Well, if somebody is in the rural area of the country where the cost of living is very low, their automotive rates might be only $80 an hour. Well, then you can start at $40 an hour for Gunsmithing and move up from that depending on demand. Remember you should also make money on parts and additional services.

So what a particular gunsmith makes is all over the place. Some people are happy only making an extra $1,000 a month as a small part-time, semi hobby-business working on just 10 to 20 guns a month. Other Gunsmiths who work at it full time and do very high-end work, can make as much as a six-figure income on an annual basis. It's not the norm, but it is possible and totally up to you.

## I live in a rural area, how can I find work?

Individuals can ship guns directly to a Gunsmith pretty much anywhere in the country as long as it's not a restricted firearm of some sort, so that gives you the ability to bring in work from almost anywhere.

A lot of our Gunsmiths get guns shipped to them from all over the country. If you're doing very high-quality work and have a good reputation and you advertise, you can get work from all over the country. For example, customers living in California or New York or other high cost of living places can legally send their guns to you and receive them back via UPS or the USPS. They often have a higher cost of living, so sending work to you often becomes very affordable to them.

And if you want to be even more specialized doing work such as; antique restoration, Gunsmiths like Doug Turnbull, have made an entire business out of restoring firearms and case hardening and so on. Many Gunsmiths specialize in building custom 1911s, or custom

Glocks, or competitive ARs, or whatever type of firearm they decide that they enjoy working on.

Specialization is another way to increase what you're able to charge, plus you make money on parts as well. But it still requires that you possess that core Design, Function and Repair knowledge.

## Do you have a list of where to get parts and would we have access to it?

Yes, we do. In fact, as part of the Professional Gunsmithing Course, we not only provide you with a list of parts suppliers, AGI also provides you with a set of thick parts catalogs totaling over 2,000 pages with schematics and part numbers for hundreds of models of guns.

Also, there are lists, links and resources, on the Gunsmithing Club of America website. **www.GunsmithingClubofAmerica.com**

## Chapter Ten

# QUESTIONS ABOUT THE AMERICAN GUNSMITHING INSTITUTE

## How long has the American Gunsmithing Institute been teaching Gunsmithing?

The American Gunsmithing Institute (AGI) was established in 1993 as a better way to teach Gunsmithing to individuals throughout the United States.

## How old do you have to be to enroll in AGI's Gunsmithing Courses?

You need to be over 18 years of age, or have an endorsement from your parent or guardian. We've had people as young as 13 and as old as 85 enroll in AGI's Gunsmithing Courses.

## Could you please describe a student's access to the instructors while you are taking the courses?

Students have access to Gunsmithing Instructors by phone and email. We also provide student forums and webinars. Also, when you enroll, you get a year of free membership in the Gunsmithing Club of America (GCA) which is a community where Gunsmiths help each other with problems, provide solutions and answer questions. This provides additional continuing education for our students.

Currently on the Gunsmithing Club of America website, there almost two hundred complete disassembly and re-assembly video courses that will help you with guns not specifically covered in the Professional Gunsmithing Courses.

## Does the information ever get outdated? What if new models of Guns come along?

Firearms utilize many of the same general systems even if they appear to look different. For example: The Military adopted the 1911

.45 Auto Pistol over 100 years ago and the ones being sold today are virtually the same as they were then. They still use the same types of systems. Once you learn the core systems that firearms use; feeding, locking, extraction, ejection, firing pins and strikers, disconnectors, sear and hammer engagement, etc. You will be able to analyze and understand any new firearms when you see them.

We created a Gunsmithing course to teach you how to understand all the systems that are relevant today and will still be relevant tomorrow and for long after that.

## What does the Gunsmithing Course cover?

The core of AGI's Gunsmithing Course is 168 hours of training in pistols and revolvers, shotguns of all action types, centerfire rifles of all action types, and rimfires of all action types.

What is really unique is we teach Design, Function, and Repair. We use cutaway guns to teach you about each of the internal systems that firearms use to operate. When you learn all the systems, you literally should be able to pick up any firearm, even one you've never seen before, and be able to analyze it and understand; what type of locking system it uses, the kind of feeding system it uses, the sear system, firing mechanism, and so on.

So as you look at those systems and say to yourself; "OK. Got it. I understand what type of systems this firearm is using. I know the rules that it operates under. So where's the stoppage? Ah yes,

I understand where and why the breakdown is happening, this is what I need to do to correct that!" That's Gunsmithing. If you don't understand Design, Function and Repair, you aren't a Gunsmith, you are just a part swapper.

That is what an armorer is. They're just a part swapper. They can take care of basic problems as long as they follow a factory list of problems and solutions. When a gun is broken, they will put in a new part, see if it fixes the issue, and if it doesn't, then; "Oh, that doesn't work. Send it back to the factory." That's the knowledge and skill level of an armorer.

We are Gunsmiths. Gunsmiths can make firearms from scratch. I mean, give us a pile of metal and we can make a gun. We understand design and function so we can look at a firearm, understand the systems and be able to make that appropriate repair. That is exactly what Master Gunsmith Bob Dunlap and the American Gunsmithing Institute, uniquely developed a systematic method to teach.

By learning firearms systems, when you go from the 1911, which uses a pivoting link system for the locking of the barrel, to then studying the Browning High-Power that uses a cam lock system, you can see and understand the differences. Our teaching method is a "building block" approach. So as we teach you each type of system one builds on top of the other, that is how you will quickly learn all of the various different systems. As we introduce each model or type of firearm, we are able show and explain to you the things that are different, thus not having to go over and over the things are exactly the same. This saves you time and is a significant shortcut to becoming a qualified Gunsmith.

## Do you teach machining skills as well?

AGI has developed a comprehensive machine shop course that takes a beginner and provides them the knowledge to safely work with machine tools. Our Machine Shop Course course covers the Lathe, Mill and general machine shop equipment. Our instructor explains all aspect of using an lathe including what to look for in a new or used lathe when purchasing one specifically for Gunsmithing. He shows you step by step how to set up and preform all the common tasks used in Gunsmithing including; threading, knurling, boring, turning, reaming, etc. Next, we teach you all aspects of using a milling machine including set-up and how to use a digital readout to make parts.

After extensively covering the Lathe and the Mill, we teach you all about the support machine shop equipment you would use in an advance Gunsmithing Shop. The Machine Shop Course is very comprehensive and yet it requires less than 30 hours of video to teach you all of that.

We utilize close-up video can see what you'd couldn't see in the first row of a regular classroom. We also take the time to show you what a proper cut or turning looks like and what the wrong way looks like so you can tell the difference.

## Do I need to know how to weld to be a good Gunsmith?

You can do a lot of different aspects of Gunsmithing and repair numerous problems without ever having to weld on a part. However, when you start doing advance repairs and restoration, I really recommend that you do learn how to TIG weld and with AGI's welding course, it really isn't that hard to acquire those skills, even if you have been frustrated by trying to weld in the past.

When you try and learn welding in a traditional shop class it is really hard. Because you really can't look over an instructor's shoulder and learn as it is just too hard to see what is going on. An instructor can't hold your arms or hands and really teach you how to weld either. So to teach welding, we created a unique process using special camera lenses and filters. That way when you see the molten puddle filling up the whole TV screen and you see the movement of the torch tip, the addition of the filler rod and the control of the molten puddle, you will quickly say "Oh, O.K., now I see it. I got it!"

The AGI welding course starts by teaching the basics with gas welding. We then take you all the way through stick (ARC), MIG and TIG. Showing you specifically how to effectively use TIG welding for gunsmithing. The beauty of TIG welding is that you can control the amount of heat you apply to the part and are able to add small amounts of metal right where you want it. The course also teaches you about gas and plasma cutting.

## Why do you think your teaching method is better than other Gunsmithing Schools?

Every one of our courses was designed with the idea of accomplishing several important things:

We wanted to preserve this knowledge for the next generation of Gunsmiths, because we realized that a great deal of it would be lost if we didn't.

We wanted to eliminate all the wasted time that results from the inefficient methods used by all campus based schools.

We realized that many people really wanted to become Gunsmiths, but they just couldn't give up their job and move to go to a gunsmithing school spending two and a half years there without an income.

Therefore, we decided to create a systematic process for teaching Gunsmithing consistently and fast, without wasting our student's time or them having travel.

Since we were highly motivated to change all of those educational shortcomings, what we now teach is far better than the instruction that I received years ago attending a campus based Gunsmithing school.

Through the use of video instruction AGI has condensed the time required to become a successful Gunsmith. One idea is presented and builds on the next. There aren't big gaps in the learning cycle like in a traditional trade school, where you learn a small piece on Tuesday and then on Thursday you're given the next little piece, and then at the same times over the next weeks you might continue to get some more bits and pieces, and so on, until ultimately you have to connect all those little pieces of information together yourself and hope that you didn't miss anything. With AGI if you are not sure about something, simply rewind and watch the video again.

Our instructors each have tremendous amounts of expertise and experience, and they're willing to share all of that with you, revealing all their secrets. Why? Because as Gunsmiths they are already in high demand and doing very well for them, they're not worried about you going into competition with them. Instead they are generous and desire to preserve this knowledge and teach the next generation of Gunsmiths to become successful.

## What is the amount of time it would take to become a certified gunsmith through AGI's course?

We've had people go through the entire course and get their certificates in as little as 90 days. But the average is six months to a year. It really depends on how motivated you are and how much time you have available to study. We do have some students that plan on doing Gunsmithing as a future retirement income and so they might decide to take several years to complete their studies. Because the course is self-paced and home study, when you complete it is really up to you.

However, let me warn you. The Professional Gunsmithing course is not something where you're just going to watch the video once and then casually check the boxes on the tests. In fact, our tests are purposely tough. Part of the reason for that is we don't want you to be a "test taker" that just looks up the answer and fills in a box. We want you to *know the systems* and be able to *think through the problems*. After completing the Professional Gunsmithing course, you should be able to do a forensic analysis of what's happening inside of any firearm. When you can do that, you will have become a real Gunsmith.

## Is it a good idea to become an apprentice to a gunsmith if I could find one to work for?

Maybe. I worked with gunsmiths in some shops that got trained at other schools and they did not truly understand design, function, and repair. Other than the basics, I ended up having to do most all of the work in the shop. Another problem is that there are good gunsmiths that you could work under, but most of them they really don't know how to teach. Or don't want to.

## If I can purchase broken firearms, is that something to start learning with?

There's certainly a lot you can learn by buying broken guns and repairing them as you are studying the Gunsmithing course. You can go to Gun Shows or pawn shops or advertise, saying "I'm a Gunsmithing Student and I want to buy broken guns to practice on." You will get some great deals!

## Does the American Gunsmithing Institute offer any hands-on training?

What our students have found to be most important is the video instruction that provides them with a complete understanding of how firearms are intended to work, along with when and how to do common repairs. The knowledge allows you to direct your hands to do the proper work even if you don't have much mechanical experience.

But in addition to the video training, AGI has developed a series of weeklong, hands-on, advanced, small group, classroom based intensive courses for the students who have completed the course.

## What if I can't afford the entire cost of enrollment at one time?

Talk to an AGI Student Advisor and they can describe the various payment options available to you including a monthly payment program.

## If I am working on a gun and I need to review a section of the course, how can I do that?

The American Gunsmithing Institute's entire Professional Gunsmithing course is indexed. So if you need to review information for a specific firearm or system, or maybe later when you've gone through the whole course, you can use your index to go back and search for a quick refresher.

## Chapter Eleven

# KIND WORDS FROM GREAT STUDENTS ABOUT AGI

We're so lucky to have incredible people come to AGI to learn the art of gunsmithing and, consequently, to open a new chapter in their lives. It may seem grandiose for me to say that the AGI courses are life-changing, so I thought I'd let our graduates speak for themselves. Thanks to AGI they are achieving their goals and exceeding them. Thanks to our students and their support, we get to achieve our goals of teaching an art form we love and creating a community that provides a valuable service.

Here's what some of our students had to say:

## "The Freedom I Enjoy Being Self-Employed is Priceless"

"I am taking a few moments out of my busy schedule to respond to your survey. After all, I wouldn't be so busy if it wasn't for your Professional Gunsmithing video course I purchased two years ago. Up until then I worked as a tool maker and CNC machinist for a large company manufacturing reduction gears and units. Punching in and out every day for a wage that allowed nothing for savings and every dime for bills. Within one short year I opened up my own firearm repair and custom refinishing shop. The knowledge I acquired through this course eliminated years of trial and error methods to achieve my goal and my love of working with firearms. My new business is exceeding my dream. My reputation among my customers is outstanding. The freedom I enjoy being self-employed is priceless. After participating in my towns regular gun shows the reviews I received were and are rewarding. Without the opportunity that AGI's course offered my dream would be just that – a dream."

— ROBERT T. BRISKEY

## "This is an EASY Way To Learn"

"The Professional Gunsmithing Course, Machinist Courses, Armorers Courses, and the other courses offered are very thorough, informative and humorous. This is an easy way to learn. You see what the professionals teach and do and then you do it yourself. You also review at will . . . In Summation, what you have is a First Class Company, with First Class Instructors, and First Class Employees, especially the ones you will work with on the phone. You won't go wrong."

— DENNIS MURPHY

## " . . . This Impressed Him Beyond Belief . . ."

"I have already fixed some guns that were repaired by our couple of local so called "gunsmiths." Including one of my own, a Browning A5 that I had the safety reversed back to right handed. I had to replace the trigger spring from a 2 prong to a 3 prong spring that is used with the cross bolt safety. Apparently the "gunsmith" did not know the difference.

Once again this is the difference between a parts replacer and a real Gunsmith. I have learned so much from the AGI course, that I can already see the difference in my education compared to the folks up here. I have a friend who had a trigger job done on his Kimber and it sometimes would "double" on him. He took it to 3 different "Gunsmiths" to have it fixed and all failed. He found out I was into this field and brought it to me. I not only diagnosed it while he was here but, promptly corrected the problems.

This impressed him beyond belief and has helped generate other business. This once again shows that it is hard to beat a good education. I look forward to retiring in VA. and after talking to many locals I have found out that the only good gunsmith within a hundred miles passed away some years ago. This will allow me to fill that void.

I look forward to my continued education from AGI and enjoy my Silver Member status in the Gunsmithing Club of America. Once again thanks to all at AGI. To know where my knowledge was just a year ago to what I have learned now is a true credit to you folks."

**— LEO WATSON**

## "The Confidence to Work On Most ANYTHING . . ."

"I recently had an experience in fixing a revolver for a gentleman who was told by the so called "master gunsmith", who works at the largest local gun outlet in town, that the gun could not be fixed. I started the AGI professional course and even before the course completion I started fixing guns. I am retired and run my small gunsmithing business because I like guns, grew up with guns in my family, and I like to compete in IPSC and SASS Cowboy action shooting in our local club. I told the gentleman I could fix his gun and I did. Test firing the pistol proved that it was fixed.

From my perspective, Bob Dunlap's knowledge about guns and how they work, and his masterful teaching methods, along with AGI's great presentations in the lessons, are far superior to what is being taught by regular Gunsmithing schools. Witness the so called "gunsmith" this gentleman first encountered who was a graduate of one of those schools.

I have to say that after years of gunsmithing using Bob's method that "if you understand how the gun works, you truly can fix it." I have experienced fixing guns from competition to many old firearms that required making parts such as "V" springs and heat treating to make a shotgun functional. Because of Bob Dunlap and AGI, I have the confidence to work on most anything that comes into my shop. Thank you AGI."

— BRUCE PROCTER, KOFA ENTERPRISE, LLC.

"I enrolled in the A.G.I. Video Course about 2 years ago. Use them as a cross-reference to complement the gunsmithing program I had attended at a college. Bob Dunlap is an excellent instructor!"

— BEN KEITH MCFADDEN, GASTON, NC

"To augment my income I enrolled and completed another course that left a multitude of questions unanswered. I then purchased the entire course that A.G.I. offered and what a difference! Just recently a customer brought in an A.H. Fox SXS that had been at another shop for 6 months without being repaired. By chance I was watching one of the Shotgun Videos and Mr. Dunlap was explaining the exact problem and how to repair it! As of this Summer I will be going full time. Thanks!"

— DAVID A. SAYERS, GOLDSBORO, NC

"I have to tell you that it is even better than a classroom, as I have the videos to fall back on when needed. My shop is doing very well."

— ROBERT DICKENS, PLEASANTON, KS

"I started Longbow Custom Firearms LLC last October. Since then, I have worked it part time, it is doing well. The biggest reason is the confidence the courses have given me, to do things I would never have tried before. The design and function knowledge I have gained is priceless. My college training was as a mechanical engineer. Four years of college did not give me the same level of insight in to mechanics that over 100 hours of quality video time with Mr. Dunlap did. Again, thank you for all your help." Sincerely,

— MIKE BLAKESMITH

## "Looking Forward to Retiring as a Part-Time Gunsmith!"

"I am a traveling professional, retired Navy and have picked up the Pro Course from A.G.I. I plan to retire in 3 years (second time), and thought the Pro-course would enable me to prep for a small gunsmithing operation. Very pleased with my investment. Bob Dunlap goes through 136 different models and covers in complete detail the design, function, troubleshooting, repair, complete disassembly and reassembly.

I do not have the time to spend in school full time. This course enables me to acquire the knowledge and as a reference value alone, it is well worth the investment to me. As I spend a lot of time away from home in hotels on the road, I have been able to go through so far 46 of the 56 videos, have taken the Pistols, Shotguns, and .22's tests.

When you consider that I got it only 6 weeks ago, I would suspect that couldn't be replicated in any other school or college. Already have worked on a couple Remington 1100's with feeding/firing problems. One was taken to a "gunsmith" locally who said the gun was "shot out" and could not be repaired . . . This "gunsmith" has been in business for 18 years. After watching the video course, I quickly fixed it with a couple of parts and a little metal bending. Looking forward to retiring as a Part-time Gunsmith!!"

— GEORGE HOWARD, ORANGE PARK, FL

"The video education is excellent. The detail and attention are better than a classroom experience. I have already done some minor Gunsmithing. I enjoy doing it. Although it is not yet a source of income for me yet. I can't imagine doing anything else."

— KYLE SWENSON, BLUFFTON SC

"I must say I thought I knew a lot about firearms but this course proves me wrong. The courses are well put together and I like being able to go back and watch a section again if I think I missed something. I have always been into guns my whole life and having my wife supporting me along this path and your well designed course of study I am realizing that what I have always enjoyed and liked to do, can become a career and a path to the way out of the factory I've worked in for the last 14 years. Thanks for your great courses."

— FRANK BACON

## "I've had an interest in firearms since I was a kid."

My brother & I built an indoor BB gun range in our basement to shoot our GI Joes & I once got in some trouble plinking sparrows off our neighbor's ham radio tower (not smart). I joined the NRA & started reading to increase my knowledge & gradually started to gravitate more toward personal & home defense firearms rather than hunting per se. I'm getting close to retirement in 2-3 years or less if I can swing it & was looking for something to keep me busy & provide additional income. I got to thinking that Gunsmithing would be a perfect choice.

So, I started looking at several options & finally settled on AGI because it seemed you folks had the most comprehensive program for what I wanted. I decided it was time to "bite the bullet" & go "all in" & ordered the entire Master Gunsmith Program (welding & machining modules included). All I can say is, "You guys rock!"

I got all my materials in just a few days & everything was as described & better. I've listened to several of the CD series already (How To Get Your FFL & Business Success Systems & Business Success Toolbox). I completed the Introductory Gunsmithing course & am almost through the Pistolsmithing section. The content is great & every question I've had has been handled quickly & efficiently by your staff. I plan to start w/ gunsmithing at home as soon as I get my FFL. Then early next year I plan to open a full service personal & home defense gunshop with my wife & youngest son after he gets out of the Army (Asymmetric Warfare Instructor – Ft. Benning, GA). Eventually we want to have an on-site training facility & indoor range. AGI has been & will continue to be a big part of making it happen! Thanks again"

— JIM RIECH

"I am a retired mechanical engineer turned part-time gunsmith via the course from AGI. During the time since I completed the professional course last spring I have obtained my FFL & provided service to gun owners repairing and restoring their firearms. I have been surprised that I have been able to determine the issue by applying the "how it works" concept Bob Dunlap teaches and make the required repairs. In a nutshell . . . I'm having the time of my life! There is nothing I have done in my previous "career" that tops the satisfaction I get being able to provide a service to my local customers and being able to fix, restore or just simply clean their firearms. I recently traded 20 steel T fence posts for a Marlin 94 in 25-20 Cal with my neighbor. The Marlin wasn't much better than the fence posts I traded for it . . . might have been one itself at some point. Now it's a fully restored & operational firearm again, resurrected from sure death! All due to valuable training I received from AGI!"

— BOB MANTHEI

"My name is James Minor, I enrolled in your Master Gunsmith course finished all of the courses except the Machine shop course which I hope to finish this year. I opened a shop and have been so overwhelmed with repairs that it has taken me time to finish the course. By the way, in the last year I have made enough money to buy a 12x36 lathe, a nice mill, a blast cabinet, a large air compressor and a nice drill press. I'm on my way! Thank you for the course. You read about this in your ads, but didn't believe it. Now I do."

— JAMES MINOR, GRANVILLE GUN WORKS

"I retired from Nissan after 26 years working as a maintenance technician in the Smyrna, TN plant. There appeared to be only a few gunsmiths in our area with very big backlogs. I felt Gunsmithing to be an area where I could do well in supplementing my retirement.

After retiring, I contacted a friend who directed me to AGI. Before taking the course I knew nothing about firearm assembly or repair. After the course I now have the confidence to tackle almost any common repair. My first repair as a student was on a Radom P-35 belonging to a friend. I repaired a feed problem and replaced broken grips. Not long after completing the course, I applied for and received my FFL. Since then I have repaired, cleaned or restored over 60 different firearms.

I would highly recommend this class to anyone interested in repairing firearms. The course was very easy to follow and Mr. Dunlap does an excellent job of presenting the material in steps that are interesting, easy to comprehend, and remember."

—WADE D. CLEMONS, WADE'S GUNSMITH, NOLENSVILLE, TN

"It is a very thorough course in very well diversified in the teachings of most weapons."

— CHARLES M BECKHAM OF VERO BEACH FL

"I want to Thank YOU Gene once again for making my dream become a reality. I wouldn't have been nearly as motivated if it wasn't made so accessible by you and your great staff. This is VERY exciting for me . . . and I know you must like to see your students put your training to good use. It must be very rewarding for you . . . .as it is for those of us that go for the roses . . . Take care Gene, Thank you." Sincerely,

— WILLIAM MACMILLAN, MAC'S PRECISION GUNSMITHING

"I never looked at anything through a design/function process before I watched the videos. It makes a lot of sense. The nice thing about the videos is you can always go back and look at what you need to have help understanding what the problem is and what it takes to repair it. The instructions are easy to follow. The close ups make it easy to see what's going on. I'm glad I took the course."

— TERRY DAVIS, PERKINSVILLE NY

"Courses are great, really like having the videos in my library for quick reference. Seeing how parts fit together, being able to rewind and pause to examine real parts is far superior to looking at drawings in a book!"

— WAYNE TURNEY, LUFKIN

"I was not able to go away to school. Every time I would get a job working at a gun shop to try to learn gunsmithing. I was always treated as the enemy and that I was going to steal all their secrets and customers. So, when I was able to afford the cost of training, I was going to get some. I found AGI even better than any of the other full-time Gunsmith schools. After I signed up with AGI I learned very fast that I had made the right decision on where to go to get the right training. I learned more from AGI then I would have ever thought possible. AGI has given me the training and skills to be a competent and professional Gunsmith. I have worked hard to be the go-to person when it comes to gunsmiths. I currently have customers that drive over 2 hours just to have me look at their firearms and then work on them. I have customers that bring me work after it has been to a Big School gunsmith and the work was done wrong or even worse. Not only did I learn how to be a gunsmith and not a parts changer, but I have been trained on how to use a milling machine and metal lathe. I have taken that training and moved it forward to learn CNC and CAD/CAM. I owe a lot to AGI."

— JOSEPH LAJOY, PLEASANT PRAIRIE WI

"This course is perfect for the home student. I can work at it on my own time whenever time is available. Very well presented and has detailed information."

— EUGENE S BISHOP, WINDSOR ME

"There is a huge amount of very important gunsmithing information in the AGI courses. Frequently accessing an experienced professional gunsmithing mentor is a key in making money for the long term."

— KEN AUSTIN, FREELAND WA

"I graduated from a junior college in 1974 with an associate degree in gunsmithing. And have worked mostly part time in the profession since. Once I discovered the AGI courses and supplemental materials I have been able to expand my knowledge and skills on a much higher level. As a result, the growth of my business has taken off and I expect this year to be my most profitable by far."

— DWIGHT CARYL, OMAK WA

"The AGI Professional Gunsmithing Course has enabled me to turn my hobby into a successful business. After taking the course, then serving as Apprentice to a local Gunsmith, I now operate my own shop, RHODE ISLAND GUNWORKS. Thanks to AGI for a Solid Foundation!"

— JASON B. LUND, COVENTRY RI

"I badly wanted to become a gunsmith and quickly became discouraged when I researched gunsmith schooling, mainly because of the time involved to do it and the cost. I saw an ad in the American Hunter magazine on how to become a gunsmith in your own home at your own pace for far less money than it would have cost to go to a college based Gunsmithing School. As soon as I read the ad, I knew this was what I was looking for. the videos allow you to replay something if you didn't understand it the first time and re-watch it as often as you like. You don't get that at a school with a professor."

— ROMAN LAPP, PEACH BOTTOM PA

"I have always been interested in guns. When I was nearing retirement, I was wondering what I would like to do when I did retire. One day I was reading a gun book and I saw an advertisement from AGI Gunsmithing, and it hit me that Gunsmithing would be perfect for me when I retired. With AGI I could finish the Course while I worked and have an enjoyable hobby when I retired. I did complete most of the courses and am a certified Gunsmith now. I now have the option of picking and choosing which work that I want to work on, and I earn supplemental income. I will say that the video way of instruction is excellent. AGI has it down to a fine art. If at any time you have a question, you just call AGI and talk to an instructor. One great thing about the videos is that you have them for future reference to review the course. AGI also offers hands on classes that I have attended. These are great classes and the Instructors are excellent. AGI is a class act and you can't go wrong with them."

— CHUCK SMITH, YUBA CITY CA

"This is the best form of training you could ask for. The flexibility is the reason I chose this course in the first place. Thank you for your time and patience."

— MATTHEW BERG, NEW BRIGHTON PA

"I work full time for a well known Gunsmithing Shop in the Portland area. We work on everything from the old broken .22 to custom firearms to automatics. Without the design, function, repair knowledge I learned from AGI I would not have been hired or gained the trust of our Smiths."

— RONALD REYNOLDS, NEWBERG OR

"Having done intensive research prior to enrolling in the Master Level Course, I found there is no other program with the in-depth training and flexibility that AGI offers."

— AARON PACKARD, WICHITA KS

"I spent over a year trying to decide which online/ digital schooling I should attend, since my family and current occupation made attending a far away brick and mortar impossible. I wanted to better my knowledge and add a certificate on the wall, in preparation for opening my full time Gunsmith Shop. I decided to go with AGI and I have not been disappointed. Would most definitely recommend for anyone wanting to engage hobby or professional skills."

— JEREMY CLARK, SAINT JAMES MO

"In brief . . . .the coursework was very detailed . . . used cutaway and modified firearms to show the internal complexities and working mechanisms . . . the instruction explained the whys' and why nots' of process and was exactly the same as sitting front row, front most seat, in a Trade school classroom . . . exactly as I had done at the trade schools . . . The examination questions are tailored to test understanding and structured to challenge that understanding. . ."

— BRIAN P. DEEZAR, CHAMPION, ALBERTA CANADA

"I found that the information in this course will give you a way to look at things in your everyday life to make better decision, by knowing the basics you can then figure out the best way to cure issues. I did not take any of the test because I wanted the course for my information. Thank you for your continued support."

— TERRY L NAIG, AMITY OR

"With the knowledge I gained from these courses I have been able to fix and repair any problems that I have had with my own firearms and those of my close friends and family."

— JOHN GRIFFITH, HAMILTON OH

"Without this course I would not have obtained my FFL and started my part time gunsmithing business. I started with wanting this as a retirement gig, however word of mouth and I have business monthly. From cleaning, parts replacement, bluing etc. Learned it all from AGI!"

— TIMOTHY OLK, AGUANGA CA

"As a prior service marine who had plenty of background in firearms. I was blown away by the amount of knowledge that I was yet to learn. it truly opened my eyes to all the different types of systems that I had yet to come across and different ways to diagnose these problems."

— THOMAS PATRICK, MIZPAH NJ

"The instructors of the courses are very knowledgeable and thorough. Would highly recommend to anyone looking to expand their knowledge for firearms whether it be for personal or financial gain."

— BRANDON BURKE, MIDDLETOWN CT

"While I am still working toward the Master Gunsmith certification, I have completed several specialty courses. 1911 pistol smith, AR Rifle smith, Glock smith, etc. All are excellent and I would recommend them to anyone with interest in those areas."

— BRADLEY HUEFTLE, TIJERAS NM

"Learning gunsmithing was fun work. I slowly gained an understanding and confidence along the way. I was not a great machinist but can carve parts, harden and fit them just fine. I do wish I started right out of high school. Man, what I missed out on."

— ERIN SHEETZ, PEKIN IL

"These courses are excellent. I've taken other so-called gunsmithing courses but none of them compared to this one. After taking these courses I do have the knowledge to diagnose and repair any gun that happens to show up at the shop."

— DEVIN SCIRANKO, MANNS CHOICE PA

"The course is simply amazing. Bob Dunlap's instruction methodology and core structure of teaching how the device works which makes it simple to diagnose what is wrong and to fix it right the first time. Stressing safety and the right way to fix things is applicable to every mechanical and electrical device out there. The course material prepares you with the knowledge to look at a gun, even if you have never seen that model, and understand how it works and be able to determine what is wrong with it and repair it in a timely manner and safely. Having the instructors available to ask questions, as well as knowing PISCO Gunsmithing is there to cover my back should I mess something up or is beyond my present capabilities, is a huge comfort. I had looked at another gunsmithing course prior to coming across AGI, and this is hands down, without a doubt, the best course of instruction out there."

— THOMAS F MURPHY, SAINT PETERS MO

"I find that the instruction is wonderful, and the method of instruction works for me. Instructors "Show You" how to do each process and explain "Why" it is designed and functions as it does. This method of instruction gives the student the skills needed to diagnose and repair any firearm."

— DOUG SWEET, OROVILLE CA

"I found the material and presentation to be very detailed and understandable. There is a tremendous amount of information that will be invaluable as future reference material. I like that the course is advance at your own speed without time restraints. This important because I have had medical issues that prevented me from advancing as quickly as I would have liked. Everyone I have spoken to at AGI has been very professional and caring, providing a much-needed service to guys like me, keep up the good work."

— KENNETH ROZELLE, CHOUDRANT LA

"I purchased the course material a long time ago when the videos were in VHS format. I have since converted mine to video. I would just like to say that Bob Dunlap is a great instructor and I refer to the videos frequently."

— TOM PARRY, HERNANDO FL

"The AGI course material was vital to my success as an independent, self-employed gunsmith. I was able to learn the key elements of gunsmithing at my own pace. These videos also provide an important library of critical information that I can as new projects come into my shop. I highly recommend the AGI program and I keep a sharp eye out for new videos from AGI as the gun industry continues to grow and change."

— DAVID R STREET, MORENO VALLEY CA

"If you have a passion for guns and like to work with your hands, there is no better job in the world then one that you enjoy. I wish I would have done this years ago."

— JOHN MOORS, LAS VEGAS NV

"The course work provided provides the foundation for gunsmithing that any other type of degree would provide for being employed in that profession."

— RYAN HEATH, HENDERSONVILLE TN

"Before AGI I would have never attempted to disassemble even some of the simplest of guns. Now I do it with confidence and speed. Time is money!"

— ROBERT TURNER, ARCHIE MO

"AGI is a great way to get into gunsmithing the right way. The videos give you the knowledge you need to start your own gunsmithing business like I have (D&W Gunsmithing LLC) going on 7 years of success."

— DAVID BORUM D&W GUNSMITHING, MARYVILLE TN

"AGI delivers with its promise of providing top quality education to even the weakest student with up close video instruction fully reviewable without effecting others learning experience, embarrassment, humiliation. You can watch it and try until you succeed and gain confidence as you go through the program without monopolizing teachers time or creating rivalries with other students. There is nothing that can be taught in a classroom that cannot be learned by AGI's video program . . . It will only cost more, waste time, upset students and eventually teachers forced to settle problems all of which are by passed by the AGI system. I have about 90% of the AGI catalogue and have never had a complaint or issue that is negative I plan to complete the catalogue as soon as finances permit me to do so."

— JOSEPH FERRARA, DARBY PA

"AGI took care of me and made a dream come true. Even by replacing my flood-lost training materials at no cost. I stand behind them whole heartedly."

— BOBBY WALKER, DAYTON TX

"The main course material and the individual weapon lessons have trained me to make improvements and repairs to guns for myself and friends and family. It has also given me knowledge that I will be using in my retirement for a retirement income."

— EDDIE HEWITT, KINGWOOD TX

"I have been to other schools and know firsthand the excellent level of training AGI provides. I have been in business for 10 years now and it has grown exponentially every year due to the service I can offer through AGI."

— TRAVIS FOLEY, BROKEN ARROW OK

"This is a very comprehensive Pro. course on function and repair. I would most defiantly recommend this for anyone who wishes to learn Gunsmithing. I plan on taking the Master Pro. later. Thanks, AGI."

— GEORGE CUBBAGE, DOWAGIAC MI

"I have been in business for ten years; a direct result of the AGI method. The opportunity to develop, expand and apply the technical and historical knowledge of firearm designs, models, actions and mechanisms has enabled me to establish a gun repair business and build a reputation that is sought after. The video instruction enables me to view individual subject matters multiple times; you can't rewind a class lecture. Additionally, the examples and explanations of discrete mechanisms enables me to reduce the time required to diagnose the root cause of a malfunction. As important as the training is the support network of a professional community provides me with the fellowship of people who share their expertise and help, guidance and inspiration. Thank you AGI and all the instructors!"

— DUWAIN BRUNDAGE, HAYDEN AL

"I always had firearms growing up and through my adult life. I thought I was pretty knowledgeable, but this course has shown me that there is always something new to learn. I am very pleased to be learning gunsmithing with the AGI system. They start you out with identification of different systems of operation and internal parts so that you can identify how the systems work and then you can make repairs. And if you have a problem just give them a call, there is always someone there willing to help you."

— SCOTT THURSTON, WOLFEBORO NH

"Working through the course gave me the skills and knowledge to better myself."

— DEFAREST B LEVERETTE, CONYERS GA

"The instructors are top notch and give you real world instructions."

— RON HOCKINS, KEENESBURG CO

"The AGI courses are far superior then Glock and Sig on-site certified courses I have attended. The depth of information and instruction is beyond my expectations. The video or online is the most efficient training method out there."

— KEVIN EVEREST, INDIANAPOLIS IN

"Very informative best part is instruction on video and can work at your own pace. Video format allows review to assist with reference at a later date."

— WILL MITCHELL, RED DEER CA

"I began my Master Gunsmithing Course with the idea that I wanted to create a viable retirement income. My dream became a reality when I applied a TIMELINE to that dream when I enrolled in the AGI Master Gunsmith Course. Through Prof. R. Dunlap's broad knowledge base and his patented system of analyzing, evaluating and seeking a root cause for problem for every situation for every firearm, I gained a great deal of information that other local gunsmiths missed when I informally questioned them independently. Mr. Robert Dunlap and his method should have been up for nomination to "A National Treasure," as so many other countries have done with their outstanding individuals in a particular professional field of endeavor."

— BERT A. LOCKE, BELGRADE MT

"I initially took a different course through another school that took me about 3 weeks to complete, however I did not learn a whole lot from it, I did some research and found that AGI was the place to go for gunsmith training. Long story short I ordered their Master Gunsmithing course and worked on completing it well myself and my partner opened a Gunsmithing shop things went very well for the first three years grossing up to $250,000 per year. I have since moved on however none of it would have been possible without AGI."

— FLINT HELLIGSO, ASTORIA OR

"The best thing about this course for me is that it was do at your own pace. Not all students will learn this at the same pace and being able to go back and review the sections that you didn't get was great."

— KIRK DAMOTH, ALTOONA IA

"Before enrolling in my first AGI course, I tried other distance learning courses and I was left very unsatisfied. I decided to start small, taking a beginning level course and WOW! What a difference. I was actually learning. I went to take the Law Enforcement Armorer course and continued to be impressed. I finally took the plunge and bought the Enhanced Master Level Professional course. It wasn't easy. I have a master's degree plus professional training in Information Technology, so I know what tough training is. I wanted to be prepared for retirement from the

Government, and AGI did just that. I got my FFL and bought a garage full of tools, including a TIG welder. Business started slow but soon I had more work than I could handle. Unfortunately, after several years, my physical problems caused by 20 years in the Army and jumping out of airplanes caught up to me. But I and still at it but at a much slower pace. I specialize in military guns used in CMP/NRA matches."

— ANTHONY MARAVOLA, GRAYSLAKE IL

"The instructors at AGI, have a passion for Gunsmithing, and the experience. I wouldn't be surprised if Bob went to sleep with his favorite rifle nearby. lol. The whole staff is about doing it right the first time. I wouldn't have been able to take gunsmithing without going online due to location, Online it's up to you to go as far and fast as you want, if you fail it wasn't because the school failed you, it's because you failed you, the support is there all the way to the top guy. Thank you AGI."

— GREG CHUTE, CHENEY WA

"I started my education with AGI so that I could have a source of income once I retired from my IT job. I was hoping to be able to finish my studies and start working on the side to build a gunsmithing business while finishing my last 10 years of employment as an IT Director. After finishing the majority of my courses with AGI I decided to leave my job 9 years earlier than I had originally anticipated. I have been running Strange Gunsmithing now for only about 10 months and in addition to our general repair and refinishing services we are working with manufacturers to produce our own line of high quality 1911's. AGI's style of teaching, via videos as well as the hands-on courses I took with Ken Brooks, have more than prepared me for my business, they have changed my life, and for the better. We have produced some 1911's and introduced them at five gun shows so far. The response has been incredible. Without the education I received from AGI I never would have been able to accomplish such a feat. With the early success we have experienced as a company, I expect great things for 2020. To all of you at AGI I give my heartfelt thanks and especially to Ken Brooks, Bob Dunlap, and Gene Shuey. You have all helped to change my life for the better. If anyone is looking at starting a career or hobby in gunsmithing, I cannot recommend the courses from AGI enough. Thanks again AGI!!"

— MICHAEL STRANGE, PRESIDENT STRANGE GUNSMITHING, HEBER CITY UT

"I coached kids in American trap and when they would have gun issues, they would take their guns to the same gunsmith who would charge them a minimum of $50 to replace parts that would not fix the problem. So, I would end up fixing them correctly because I understood the design and function of the firearm. I have a good mechanical and problem-solving mind, but the AGI instructors explain it so well that it is very simple to understand, and if I happen to struggle with it, I back up the video and watch it again. This is an outstanding school teaching solid gunsmithing principles the correct way. We are problem solvers not parts swappers!"

— MIKE CUMBERWORTH, VERSAILLES IN

"I took AGI after the VA said I was disabled and unemployable. I fell into depression and AGI brought meaning back into my life. Now own my own shop and in the process of hiring an employee to help with the workload."

— JOSHUA TOLBERT, RAGLEY LA

"AGI courses will prepare you to be a gunsmith as well as any of the traditional in class courses. I know this because I know a few people that attended and completed the gunsmith course at Lassen College. Talking with them I feel I received as good of an education as they did and I'm not thousands of dollars in debt. In fact, none of those Lassen graduates are even gunsmithing anymore, at least not around here. I can attest to the course's ability to prepare a person to become a gunsmith, as well as getting an FFL and other details. Highly recommended course for anybody wanting to get into gunsmithing."

— JASON CARDINALE, PASO ROBLES CA

"I have finished the course but haven't turned in all exams. This course has enabled me to do many tasks very successfully. Without the videos to refer to I would not have the close at my fingertips any time of day or night that it provides over and over on any firearm subject or problem. It is downright stupid not to have all this info on hand to refer to at a given moment. Can even save your life and others. I will always have a mentor on hand when needed! Thank you AGI and all trainers!"

— BRUCE V MAJORS, BEDFORD IN

"The course was excellent, and I can honestly say that I use the skills I learned from your program (particularly the information from the "Introduction" section) each working day. I also found the sections on lathe, mill and other machine shop operations very helpful along my path to becoming a competent machinist. I recommend your courses to everyone that asks me about how to become a gunsmith. Thanks to everyone at AGI for their part in making my gunsmithing business a success."

— PAUL GIBERTINI, GREAT GUNS ARMORY, PLAINFIELD IL

"If you like your guns and have the mechanical aptitude and desire to work on them, these courses are great. Gunsmiths are becoming scarce.

Factory services aren't so great and can't always fill your need. I run my own shop as an LLC. The only gripe is too much junk coming in and high insurance, but I am not quitting. The course cover most of the old and new guns one sees. I am pretty confident about what I can do for my customers because of the AGI courses. I would do it all over again but earlier in life."

— JOHN FERRELL, NEW RIVER GUNSMITH, FAIRLAWN VA

"I took the course prior to retiring to supplement my income. After 3 years working part time for myself as a gunsmith I decided to fully retire."

— ALAN FULLMER, IDAHO FALLS ID

"The course has given me the confidence to work with all types of firearms. I have been able to find information in the materials to help me disassemble repair or modify and rebuild every firearm I have been presented with."

— MATTHEW SNYDER, CARLSBAD CA

"Although I have been a Police Armorer for more than 25 years, the courses I have completed through AGI (Law Enforcement Armorer) has enhanced my knowledge on a multitude of firearms. The courses covered not only the types of firearms normally issued to Law Enforcement Officers, but also many that are carried by Officers off duty."

— AL AMORE, CANYON COUNTRY CA

"Excellent course well thought out and presented in an easy to follow format."

— BUTCH MADDOX OF TROY NC

"This course was a life saver for me. I had surgery and an accident shortly after starting the course. I was able to retire early and still have a decent income. It also helped me fulfill a childhood wish, being a gunsmith. While I'm still completing the course, I am able to work in the areas I've completed."

— P. GARY FERRERO, MURRAY UT

"This course is how I learn the best. I studied the 911 portion along with all the other 911 courses and now have the slickest Kimber 911 in the city. Awesome!"

— TIMOTHY PERREAULT, IGNACIO CO

"Great course I was a small arms repair in the army. I learned much more with the AGI program."

— STEVEN WILLIAMS, LEXINGTON SC

"This course is a comprehensive and extremely well-planned instruction. EVERY level and EVERY course is expertly done. I would watch the video then repeat it with a firearm in front of me and go through it while I did what the instructor doing. I could stop the video replay the video or start completely over if I needed to. It was great. This methodology was amazing. I cannot say enough positive statement about it. Thank you AGI for all the extremely hard work to make learning easy and very enjoyable."

— KEVIN BRADLEY, SPRINGFIELD MO

"The AGI video gunsmithing course is an excellent program. It is nice to be able to roll back, rerun and revisit parts that are giving you a problem. Once you are working as a gunsmith it is nice to be able to go to these videos and refresh yourself if you're having an issue with a gun that you are having trouble resolving. You will learn from these videos . . . Thank you AGI for giving me the knowledge to work as a gunsmith."

— TOM LOIMO LMBERT AND SMITHERS GUN SHOP, REDWOOD CITY CA

"This AGI course prepared me for a very successful occupation as a gunsmith. It's been a great reference when I've had questions. I am currently well-known with a good reputation and I'm doing very well as a gunsmith. I have recommended this course to many of my friends."

— ADAM JEPPSON, MOUNT PLEASANT UT

"I enrolled in AGI to learn basic gunsmithing skills. When I received my materials, I was blown away by the incredible amount of information. To be honest it was a little intimidating. However, the instructions provided we're well above industry standards and Bob Dunlap (God rest his soul) taught in a way that it was like having him in the same room."

— BRIAN CUTHBERT, BLUE RIDGE VA

"I wanted to find something I could do after being retired. I decided to do gunsmithing because that has been a love of mine. It was something I could do with my particular disease. The courses taught me the fundamentals that were needed to do the work. The test was hard, you had to pay strict attention to the information given. These courses taught the systems that firearms work off of. It is not a gun specific course. These classes teach the theory of how guns operate. once these theories are learned, it will lead to fixing several of firearms that operate with that same theory of operation. Before I had to retire, I was an instructor for both Fire and EMS classes. The fundamentals are key. AGI's classes teach the fundamentals!!! I have been able to repair firearms that I have never seen before and then been brought other firearms of that type because the original customer was so happy that they told others. This is a CLASSIC course!!! The support after you finish the course is incredible!! I have run into issues that I was not sure about. I went back to the classes and called the support staff and have been able to resolve every issue. Resulting in a firearm that has worked perfectly. This is a program that does what it says it will do!!!"

— JACK HINDS, GLEN ROSE TX

"I took the AGI Master Gunsmithing course after becoming Disabled and confined to a bed most of the time for 3 years and 2 1/2 years of Physical therapy learning to walk again. While starting this course it led me to starting Community College to learn Machining after starting the AGI Master Gunsmithing program. With the knowledge from AGI's machining course I excelled and became Student of the year as well as making Dean's list and President's list at my community college. AGI helped me find self-worth again after I had almost lost it after becoming Disabled and struggled with what direction I would take in life. I highly recommend AGI's and ATI's courses and can't say enough or recommend them enough."

— DONALD W. BARROW, CORPUS CHRISTI TX

"The training has helped me to understand and analyze other systems that I work on. It taught me the importance of effective organization, and record keeping."

— MARK E. DAVIS, LANSING MI

"Gunsmithing for me is a hobby but the knowledge and skills I have gained has made me invaluable to many shooters, hunters and gun owners in general. With the knowledge I gained through the AGI program I have never been presented with a gun I could not repair, including guns that other gunsmiths said they could not repair. I assume because they couldn't buy the parts needed and lacked the knowledge to repair or make the parts themselves (Knowledge I gained from AGI). I am proud of what I do and intend to turn my hobby into a business and career very soon. Thank you AGI for giving me the knowledge, opportunity and confidence to pursue that dream."

— SCOTT MORROW, OAKVILLE WA

"Has been a good base of training that I've used over and over for repair work. Great help and source of extra income."

— KEVIN ANTHONY, BOISE ID

"Course gave me the knowledge and confidence to do gunsmithing without the fear of being a failure. I learned about how all the parts inside are supposed to work together to allow firearm to function like it is supposed to. Also, about making a part and tempering or casehardening it, and a tremendous amount more information than I have room to wright. Well worth the money."

— CHIS SMITH, RICHLAND GA

"Great format, easy to understand and great close ups. I have attended armorers' courses in person but never got the views of what was being worked on like I did through AGI's courses."

— HARRY NOLAN, RIGBY ID

"I have always done my own disassembly and cleaning of my personal firearms. I thought I knew a little about firearms. When I started the AGI courses I soon realized that's all I knew was a little. After going through the courses that teach design and function my knowledge of different firearms has drastically increased because I now know how they work. With most firearms that I work on now, I have a good idea of the problem just from the customer describing what the firearm is doing or not doing. The reason I can do this is because the instructors at AGI has educated me in the design and function of firearms. If I know how it works, I can fix it."

— JERRY DEWAINE STANFILL, EL DORADO AR

"I got this course after being laid off from a sales organization after 12 yrs of service. Previous to that, I was a law enforcement officer in a large municipality for about 15 yrs. I have always had a desire to get into Gunsmithing but never had the opportunity. The sudden loss of employment gave me the boot in the pants I needed to switch careers and I found work at a local gun shop. I purchased the AGI Professional Gunsmithing program to supplement my income and provide more in-depth training for my new career path. I was also looking for a part time job that I could fall back on as I approach my retirement years. I've found the course material to be quite relevant and very helpful to me. The knowledge of Master Gunsmith Bob Dunlap and the other instructors is unparalleled and has been most helpful in my new direction. I would recommend this course to anyone unable to attend a brick & mortar institution and pay the tens of thousands of dollars such an education would cost."

— JIM LONG, HONOLULU HI

"AGI is the best school for firearms repairs they teach it correctly. I started acquiring courses as I could afford them while still working. As retired now and building a new house with a great shop will be finishing the schooling, I have invested in. Having been with AGI from very close to the start the knowledge that has been acquired and not even had time to complete my courses as of yet is PRICELESS! If you would like to learn it right go with AGI!"

— MICHAEL E MILES, LEXINGTON SC

"The videos gave me the confidence I needed to plunge in knowing what you can and cannot do. I would recommend this system for any kind of teaching and learning, not just gunsmithing. I could learn at my pace and play it over and over till it sunk in."

— RANDY DREYER, DORR MI

"I found AGI while my wife was working in Australia on a two-year assignment. I started with the basic course first to see if it was a good fit. After working through the basic course, I was very impressed with the content and the Instruction. I then purchased the Professional course. After completing that I went for the master level course. I have since opened a gunsmithing business that I am running from my home until I have enough business to open a shop at another location. I've always felt the best way to repair/build something is to know how it works first. That is the main reason I went with AGI training. Thanks for an excellent format for learning."

— MICHAEL DUECKER, LEXINGTON SC

"I have signed up for the level 2 gunsmithing course. I haven't finished yet but that is my fault. I had to take time for my primary job. I have completed a section and feel like I have learned enough to work on most pistols and shotguns. I have bought several of their other courses like triggers, Armorer courses, and bluing videos. All of those are top notch and I have learned so much from them. I actually started to work part time using what I learned from them. I believe once I finish the other courses in the level 2 course, I will be making more money. I truly believe that it is the next best thing to a brick and mortar school."

— GUSTAVO MORALES, BROOKSVILLE FL

"Because having gained the necessary knowledge from this course, I have opened my part time business called Aim Focus and Fire, LLC. on April 15, 2019, I have my 001 FFL, and have been selling firearms and fixing firearms. I have also fixed a few rifles that some other gunsmiths were not able to repair, and I didn't even get a chance to finish the rifle coarse yet. It shows there is a lot of knowledge to be learned from the pistols, shotguns and rimfire courses and the note booklets that can be helpful when working on rifles. Actually, I was able to fix the rifles because the procedure to fix the problems were in there."

— KEITH ROMERO, YOUNGSVILLE LA

"These Master Gunsmith, Machine Shop and Professional Welding courses, are on par and exceeds the technical training, I received at a local city College in San Diego, which also focused attention on the concept of Design, Function, and Repair of Industrial Flexible Manufacturing and Robotics Systems and Electronic and Mechanical Equipment. (also, an excellent course) My previous experience with the concept of Design Function and Repair got my attention and led me to investigate AGI, and its program. The video lessons and the ability to instantly review difficult concepts and visually review them, and if necessary, to call the advisors with specific questions, has been invaluable to me and I am sure to others with limitations. AGI's approach and program met my individual needs better than any other gunsmith school that I researched. I am not disappointed with the at all."

— RANDALL PHILLIPS, EL CAJON CA

"The backup and support of the school was and is outstanding. When I have a problem that I can't solve I can get assistance from AGI staff to help me."

— STEVEN J YBARRA JD, SACRAMENTO CA

"I know it seems like you could never afford the course, but you need to do whatever it takes to buy the course. If you want to be a Gun Smith this is the only way a working man can make it! Do as I do and do it in part one and move on when you have the money. I will never finish mine because of Cancer but hopefully you will not have this problem. Go for it I had planned to do the Enhanced Master Level Three, but Doctors have taken that away."

— JAMES WESLEY RAINS, SR, ALACHUA FL

"The videos and instructors are very good I probably will not see all the videos but when I get a firearm in I'm not sure about I'll watch the video for that particular firearm and it makes it very easy just like a hands on class."

— JAMES WHITT, MUENSTER TX

"Excellent course and Excellent instructors. Advisors and website chats are an enormous help. Very knowledgeable people, if they don't have the answer, they will find it."

— JIM BONNEY, REEDSVILLE WV

"Started my own business when I retired, and it continues to grow. The AGI videos have lots of good info for a variety of guns and is a good reference source."

— MICHAEL COMER, SIKESTON MO

"I do Restorations and Repair. Mr. Dunlap's expertise in older fire-arms has been invaluable. Anyone thinking of moving into the firearms industry should consider this course. It is well planned and well executed. Thank you all for all you have done for the industry."

— RILEY JOHNSON, BELHAVEN NC

"Great Instructors who are masters in their fields. Great instructional videos. Teaching design/function/repair."

— JAMES J VLASAK, WHITEWATER CO

"I have not started working in the craft yet; however, I get to do some family-related work (not a good business model) I have learned more about what I did not know and it is initially humbling. After the course and the knowledge gained has paid off in lowered costs for upgrades and modifications. Some not quite business appropriate in time taken but quite helpful in family finance savings."

— COREY CREVELING, SPARKS NV

"I did a good amount of research and even spoke to a former student/graduate of AGI Master Gunsmithing program prior to purchasing the course myself. I visited his shop which employed several other gunsmiths. The course was VERY challenging and required my full and undivided attention. I did not pass parts of the program on my initial attempt, (and these are "open video" exams). The program and tests are not designed to let you pass and get a feel good certificate, they are meant to give you the tools and knowledge to figure out the answers to both the exam questions but also the future gunsmith problems you will likely face. My present job requires that I have continuing education, but they are nowhere near as comprehensive and rewarding as the classes from AGI. This has been one of the most rewarding and best educational investments I have ever made. I consider my course material to be one of my prized possessions."

— GREG ZYDIAK, HERMANN MO

"Although I use the material from a hobbyist standpoint, I find the disc courses extremely helpful in the operation and take down of most commonly used firearms. I feel the course was worth the investment."

— A ROBERSON, SOMERVILLE AL

"I have consistently used the videos as a reference when I took on a project that I was not familiar with."

— JACK BROWN, PRINEVILLE OR

"After completing this training, it has given me a great since of satisfaction knowing that I can make repairs to firearms for my friends, family, and me. While I've had the opportunity to work on several guns the last few years, the idea of being able to make a little money in retirement doing something fun is what caught my attention. Thanks, AGI!"

— LAMAR DORRIS, YAZOO CITY, MS

"I bought the AGI course to learn the gunsmithing trade at my leisure. so far, I have been so busy working on my own guns and my main job and friends' guns from what I have learned in the courses so far. I have two of my friends that are thinking of ordering courses from AGI as well."

— NICK S TATARCHUK, HOLLAND MI

"Listen up folks, if you really want to learn gunsmithing, learn it from the best, American Gunsmithing Institute. Trust me, if my brain can process what's going on so can yours, I have A.D.D — attention deficit disorder, I quit school when I was 16 because I could not handle sitting in a classroom, my thought process is as scattered as it gets, and my attention span, well it's short! I'm telling you; this course is perfect for us A.D.D guys through the wonderful technology of a rewind button on the DVD player, plus you don't feel like a lost idiot sitting in a classroom! Bob Dunlap breaks it all down in simple easy to understand Design, Function & Repair lessons. But if you don't understand, rewind, watch and listen again! I went in a little bit different direction with my gunsmithing knowledge, I own a business that does specialized coatings on firearms called cerakoting. I can tell you for an absolute fact, if it was not for learning D, F & R from AGI, I would not be doing cerakoting. It's because of AGI that I have my 07 FFL manufacturers license. Go for it, you will not regret signing up for AGI's gunsmithing course!"

— DARYL MILLER, FOMBELL PA

"AGI is a tremendous resource for training and re-training yourself in the gunsmithing profession. Their products are fantastic, and the instructors are Masters of their craft!"

— RODNEY BALDRIDGE, BENTON AR

"I opened a Gun Shop 5 years ago, and I do Gunsmith work as well as buy, sell, and trade. I'm always backed up with Gunsmith work as there are very few Gunsmiths around. Other "Gunsmiths" send me work also. Thank you AGI! I couldn't have done this without you!!!"

— DAN FOX, FLORENCE AL

"This has really changed my life in a very positive way. If I had known about this when I was young, I would have made a completely different career. I truly love working on and building firearms. This to me is very exciting. I can't tell how much enjoyment it is for me to be able to repair or build a new firearm. I will truly miss Bob Dunlap and thank each and every one of you for all you do for each of the students."

— RONNIE CROUCH, LYNCH STATION VA

"I can't give AGI enough praises. I can work on anything that comes in front of me because of your training. I'll be finished with the course soon and will be opening my business hopefully this spring/summer. Thank you for helping me achieve my dream. Working full time, I couldn't afford the big local Gunsmithing school, nor had time to. But with AGI, I get to it when it fits my schedule. Thank you so very much."

— JESSE F. HUBBELL, BUTLER PA

"The course is detailed beyond my expectations and the resources are just about endless."

— ROBERT M HAYES, UKIAH CA

"The gunsmithing course is well thought out and worth the time. Thanks you for allowing me to learn a lost art."

— TED ROGUS, STEPHEN NM

"I thought the instructors were very informative and professional in their presentation of the material."

— SCOTT AICHER, LAS VEGAS NV

"The AGI course is easy to follow and learn from."

— BENJAMIN GIVEANS, WISNER LA

"The AGI Gunsmithing program goes far beyond its promise. I would recommend AGI and its programs to anyone."

— MARK BADEAUX OF MADISONVILLE LA

"Congratulations on producing the most thorough and valuable fire-arms repair program the market has ever seen. I was very skeptical when I first enrolled in the course because everything else I had previously experienced, ranged from dismal to an outright rip-off. The Fact that you teamed up with Bob Dunlap gave me the confidence that you probably had the knowledge and know-how to produce a proper and credible course.

I certainly was not disappointed; on the contrary, I was pleasantly surprised on how difficult it was. I could not even answer one question on the first page of the exams the first time I looked at them. I knew then that I made not only a good choice but also a good investment. With each video I completed and each job I repair right the "first time" I can honestly say that I am on my way to becoming an excellent gunsmith."

— WAYNE RUDRUM, CRANBROOK, BC

"I would never have expected that I could be a Gunsmith. But as of this day, I am now a Certified Professional Gunsmith thanks to everyone at AGI. I was in a terrible accident 3 years ago and suffered brain damage. But with your training and Bob's teaching ability I am now a professional Gunsmith. I won't say it was a piece of cake, but I was able to pursue my dream, even with my disability. Also Thanks to the AGI Staff for being there to guide me when I was having trouble. Once again THANK YOU to everyone that helped me reach my goal and dream of being a Professional Gunsmith. I am still not used to my new title "Gunsmith," but I still have the rest of my life to get use to it! Thanks again."

— JOHN HEISER

"The instruction is very clear and concise. The instructors are very knowledgeable."

— TILLIE FORD OF ELLSINORE MO

"If you are putting off this as you feel you don't know a particular aspect of being a gunsmith, don't worry as with this course you can go as deep or as light as you want in each area."

— JEFF REESE OF GARDEN GROVE CA

"It is a super course and I'm glad I enrolled."

— FRANK OF FRANKLINTON NC

"I love the AGI Gunsmithing course! You have taught me how it all works, and I can always go back and review something if needed. And it is needed. Thank you AGI."

— CHRIS MILES OF MESA AZ

"Recently I enrolled in the AGI Certified Firearm Appraisers course along with the Master Gunsmith course. The help I have received for some of my questions was invaluable and much appreciated. It really helped to guide me in the right direction with my thought process and even clarified the fact that I over analyze simple things.

AGI has definitely produced an amazing course thus far in my experience. I already have one appraisal that I am working on and this is while I am still waiting for my certificate to come to me! I look forward to digging deeper into the course materials and getting the most out of it all.

Please inform Gene that the interviews and the business success kit are extremely informative and valuable to someone like me just starting out. I commend you all for the high quality work being produced and distributed. Thank you all!"

— JEREMY MARCOTTE

"Things have been growing so fast, that I was curious about just how many guns I worked on last year because I am way busier this year than last. So I counted and I was a little bit surprised at how many it was…281 guns I worked on last year . But that's only the number of guns that were logged into my system because they had to stay the night as parts were made or ordered for the guns to be repaired. There were many other guns that were quick fixes and quick cash.

Mind you I have been able to do these repairs with just my LE armorer's course, practical gunsmithing course, and my pistolsmithing course, I'm in the middle of the Professional shotgun course as we speak. Anyway back to the numbers…last year almost each month grew but this year it has doubled and I love it!

Also doubling the number of guns from last year also makes me very happy I made the decision and investment to be a part of AGI and the Gunsmithing Club of America. I even just picked up my first "across" state gun for me to work on he drove almost 4 hrs for me to repair and upgrade his gun.

I couldn't have done this without the help of everyone at AGI and I greatly appreciate all the help everyone has provided me. Now I just need to find time to get my other courses completed….tough when you're a single father of two great boys and fixing all these guns but I do keep on making progress watching the videos and taking tests. Thanks Again."

— JOSHUA J STEVENS, ROGERS AR

"It is an excellent course for those who wish to be a Professional gunsmith or for the hobbyist who wants to be able to work on their own guns."

— EVERETT "BRICK" NOYES OF RIVERSIDE CA

"I still use course material as a problem-solving tool. Any time I need a hand all I do is ask the staff."

— PAT DELONG OF HELENA MT

"I have learned to be able to know how a firearm works and repair a problem NOT just throw parts at it."

— MATT WINEY, OLATHE CO

"AGI staff was fantastic to work with. Always got back with an answer to whatever question I had. Instructional videos were great, and VERY in depth. I did the program through the VA Vocational rehabilitation program, and was kind of sad when it was all over. I wanted more. I like to put random old coursework on the shop tv sometimes while I'm working, and I am constantly learning things I may have missed, or brush up on old tricks, etc. Like I said, I am always trying to learn more and more. AGI continually provides me with that."

— MATTHEW TAYLOR, GLENMOORE PA

"I have only completed some of the sections of the course but I am already actively Gunsmithing."     — DAVID PULLEN, MI

"The material covering design and function of firearms, alone is worth the expense."     — MICHAEL BLAKESMITH, LAKEWOOD OH

"I think the course material is very good. It has definitely improved my skill set. It has taught me things I did not know, as well as things I did not know I did not know."

— STEVEN W. BARTELT, TURNERSVILLE, NJ

"WOW!! Talk about making the Lathe & Mill understandable. Mr. Holland is definitely a master at his trade. He has a no-nonsense approach and gets right to the point. By the time you get through the videos you are ready to tackle almost anything."

— DANNY REJDA, LUSK WY

"Excellent Course. A Great job of combining theory, practical application and live demonstration, to create a very effective learning experience."

— JOHN EVANOO, LONDON OH

"I believe that this is the first video course that actually fulfills my expectations. This course is exceptional. As a Gunsmith, I am a beginner Lathe operator, using only book knowledge since there are no trade schools in my area and I don't know any machinists. Your video course has totally opened my eyes to the use of the Lathe & Mill. I now feel much more confident about using them."

— FRANK ROONEY, CORONA CA

"I have just completed the final section of the Machine Shop course, and as expected the information on setting up a machine shop, equipping it and the overview of some of the support equipment was excellent. As a Gunsmith who is expanding his machining capability, and is in the process of building a new workshop from the ground up, the information it contained was extremely valuable. As he did in the Lathe & Milling sections of the course, Darrell's presentation of technique and demonstration of machine set-up was outstanding. His ability to communicate the information is first rate."

— DOUGLAS SPOONER, THE ARMORER'S BENCH, ADAMS CENTER NY

"I had actually purchased my Lathe before I enrolled in this course. The lathe came with just a parts list and recommended fluids for lube. I had thousands of dollars tied up and did not know how to use it. I have ordered other how-to video courses from AGI before, so I knew you guys were the best choice for me. After watching the Lathe videos I had no trouble at all setting up my lathe and turning out all types of work. I could not have done this without the American Gunsmithing Institute! I am looking forward to a long relationship with AGI, Thank you for giving so much for the firearms industry."

— DOUGLAS PATRICK, LAUREL, DE

"As an instructor/Professor, I felt that the course was well presented and very thorough."

— DIDRIK C KROGH, ROCHESTER MI

"If I got stuck on a certain issue, help was only a phone call or e-mail away. But that was rarely needed."

— BILL TABER, BULLS GAP TN

"The best part of the AGI structure is you have a huge library of videos to go back to for refreshers."

— ROBERT D BROWN, GRANTS PASS OR

"The video courses don't just prepare you to pass the tests, they make you think logically about how your firearm(s) actually operate. With that mind frame you can repair anything."

— GARY FAGAN, GYPSUM CO

"Prepares you for being a quality gunsmith."

— PHIL DYER, WARREN OH

"I started Gunsmithing out of my garage, but moved 4 months ago to a street side store front with 1000 sq feet. I have a sandwich sign on the front side walk for now, and just the walk-in's has paid the rent ever since and then some, that is no bull... My business has increased so much that I have a 3-4 week back log, even with a helper that does all the gun cleaning and minor repairs that I oversee.

My accountant has advised me that at this rate I will just about TRI-PLE my business for the year, can't wait for next year. Thanks to AGI of course. I also have started a specialty side to my biz. Before I had to sub out all of my hot bluing, parkerizing, and welding, not any more. I do all of that in house myself, the other end of that is the Polymer frame reductions and stippling. I am starting to get these in from other states and gun shows and even my local PD, WOW see me next year, There's a lot more to tell, some other time... Thank you!"

— JAN-MERSON, AMERICAN FIREARMS & GUNSMITH, LA HABRA CA

"The AGI course material not only provides the knowledge detail necessary for the maintenance and repair of all firearms, it also provides a handy library of reference material that has helped pinpoint issues and fixes for unusual or rare firearms failures."

— JOHN WEAVER, GLASGOW KY

"I found the AGI gunsmith course offer to provide the best possible classroom instruction on a vast array of different types of firearms."

— FRANK MCGUIRK, NIPOMO CA

"As a retired military member I was looking for a profession that would build upon my love of firearms. After researching every institution that offers gunsmithing, I found that a majority of them require you to physically attend the course and none of them were close to where I live. After learning AGI was a distance learning program, talking to a few industry professionals, and deciding my goal is to eventually be self-employed, I decided to enroll in AGI's Enhanced Master Gunsmith Course. The course provided the flexibility to work at my own pace since I have to work a regular job and have family commitments. I am proud to say that I have completed the course, started my own gunsmithing business, and am on my way to becoming a full-time gunsmith."

— DAVE ROSENFIELD, LAKESIDE CA

"I presently have several welding processes available in my Gunsmithing shop for the almost daily soldering, brazing jig & fixture making, tool building and maintenance operations that are necessary for a custom shop. I have never really understood those processes until viewing your new Professional Welding Course. I enrolled in the welding course, secure in the knowledge that I would receive the same superb training I that I have come to expect from the American Gunsmithing Institute. My expectations have been exceeded! After 35 years of being disappointed with my welding skills I feel that I have finally found the knowledge that I need to improve my welding to a point on par with my other shop skills!"

— GARY IAMES, SOUTH LAKE TAHOE CA

"I am a professional pilot for a major airline and have a small firearms business on the side. Being a pilot my work schedule varies from week to week so taking a classroom welding course was not an option for me. When AGI announced that a welding course was being developed, I was excited and one of the first to enroll. I knew that if the welding course was on par with the other AGI courses I had, it was going to be good. Well, I just finished reviewing the course and it's Fantastic. I have tried gas and arc welding many times in the past. One thing for certain…I had no idea of what I was doing. And as for MIG and TIG; What's That?!?!

I had read all the manuals on gas and arc welding but I could Not convert all of the reading and photos to practical application. You can't just read about welding and expect to get good results; you need a professional instructor. This video course gives you that professional instructor. It allows you to watch the welding process up close. You can't get any closer!

Watching the welding process, as the instructor is explaining what he is doing. I don't believe you can get this level of instruction in a classroom. And best of all, if you miss something …just hit rewind and watch it again. This course Covers all the basic types of welding. Gas welding/cutting, arc, MIG and TIG but most importantly it covers Gunsmith welding. This course has made me a more confident and competent gunsmith. Well worth the investment. Thanks."

— JEFFERY C. MAY, PRESIDENT /GUNSMITH, TACTICAL TOOLS INC., OAKTON, VA

"AGI provides excellent educational materials that will give you the knowledge needed to perform Gunsmithing and other related firearm careers. I have completed a number of the courses and have a very successful Gunsmithing & Firearm Appraisal business in Tucson Arizona. I highly recommend AGI courses."

— JOE GOODALE, TUCSON AZ

"If you truly apply yourself to the "design, function, and repair" method, whenever a new weapons system is placed in front of you there will be no head-scratching. I believe AGI lays the most solid firearms foundation in the country! They have given me the knowledge and confidence to repair any firearm that a customer places on my bench."

— J ISAAC SILVERNAIL, GREELEY CO

"The design and function part of the course alone is invaluable."

— CHRIS SANDERS, TRINITY TX

"Having completed testing and certification on Level One Professional Gunsmithing course, I must say, all AGI videos are very, very thorough in teaching Design, Function, and Repair. The material also serves as the BEST reference library I have ever seen. Well done. Thanks, Gene, for having the foresight to immortalize.

— MR. ROBERT DUNLAP, CHARLES BLOCK, ORANGE TX

"I am a disabled Marine veteran. While stationed in North Carolina I apprenticed with a gunsmith for two years. The gunsmith taught me a lot about gunsmithing, much of which he learned in school. Upon receiving my disability rating from the VA, I contacted my local Regional VA Vocational Rehab office. After months of writing a business plan, and dealing with all the red tape with the VA, I was accepted into the AGI Enhanced Master course. I have never been happier.

I already had my FFL and business when I enrolled in AGI, but I needed more. AGI's Enhanced master course has not only supplied me with tools and equipment for most of what I do, but I have learned so much more in one year of the course than I did two years as an apprentice. If you are a disabled vet, and love working on guns, I highly suggest you look into this course. Having the VA pay for everything was great.

I have recently gotten to the machine shop course, and I already purchased a lathe and small mill a year before starting school, but I never really felt comfortable using either piece of equipment. After a few hours of watching the lathe course, I was turning out parts you think would come out of a master machinists shop.

Everything from firearms, machining, and welding is broken down to fully understand it all. If you think your having a little trouble, unlike a classroom, you can rewind as many times as you want until it is stuck in your head. It is certainly a course that isn't for the faint at heart, as it is not easy to just breeze through, you have to really learn it.

When you learn something from AGI, and offer that service when no one else around you does, people fly to your shop to have you do it. I offered general repair on several types of firearms, and got good business. Now that I have learned so much more and can offer it because other gunsmiths around don't/cant, business has grown so much, I can barely keep up. If you are a veteran like me, take this course and you not be disappointed. I always thought I'm getting all this education, tools, equipment, and, I am getting it for free because the VA paid for it. AGI explained to me that disabled veterans are in fact not getting it for free, they paid their dues, just not with money. Thank you AGI for making my life happy and successful once again."

— MATTHEW TAYLOR, GLENMOORE, PA. TAYLOR FIREARMS, LLC

"As a Mechanical Engineer I was surprised at the level of technical knowledge imparted by AGI and Bob Dunlap and how the course showed the application as relating to problems encountered in everyday gunsmithing."　　　　— JIM LARSON, PERKASIE PA

"I believe that the AGI pro courses are hands down the best source of information to learn Design, Function, and Repair of firearms and gives you the ability to apply that knowledge to solve any problem that comes along. The fact that all course info is on video which allows you to go back and refresh your knowledge is invaluable. Also the knowledge of safety and how a firearm must work is extremely important in maintaining or repairing a firearm to function safely. Also their continuing education articles and published information are second to none."

— LANCE CUNNINGHAM, GEORGE WEST TX

"If you understand the basic firearm the course will help every other part of gunsmithing make sense." — ALAN NAGROCKI, LAKE ZURICH IL

"Course are very informative and allow you to learn at your own pace. I've completed some courses quickly and some I've taken my time with and completed over time."

— CHRISTOPHER MELENDEZ, LIVERMORE CA

"The course brought me to a point where I could expand my knowledge on my Own, a superior base line."

— GLENN MOREFIELD, MECHANICSBURG OH

"The course gives an incredible amount of detail and it really feels like you are in the classroom with the instructor."

— MIKE KEOUGH, MONUMENT CO

"Great and well explained material. Fantastic advisors and staff. I would recommend this course to anyone!."

— ROBIB BENHAM, VERSAILLES IN

"This course has expanded my proficiency with fixing firearms."

— JOSEPH MAGYAR, PHENIX CITY AL

"I am currently building custom rifles based upon the education that I received through watching the gunsmithing training videos."

— NORMAN WEBB, DAPHNE AL

"AGI courses are an outstanding way to become a very knowledgeable gunsmith. I started with the basic hobby course, and enjoyed it so much while learning valuable skills, that I continued on with the Professional courses. After I retire from my lifelong flying career, I plan to continue with the Master Level courses to further enhance and grow my small gunsmithing business. I can't say enough about the quality of these courses, combined with the instructors and support personnel that make up AGI. They make learning the gunsmithing trade enjoyable and, most importantly, profitable. I would highly recommend to anyone considering gunsmithing as a business, or even just to further their own hobby- check out AGI! You will not be disappointed!"

— SCOTT CROSLEY, COTOPAXI CO

"Not only do you learn a trade to earn a income, but you learn about the fascinating mechanical abilities of the creators of firearms."

— DAN SHARON, BUTTE MT

"I am retiring from the carpenter trade at the end of this year and will become a full time self employed Gunsmith. I believe someone can learn a hands on trade from this video format just as I did They of course will have to practice the skills to become efficient with them. But I am proof it can easily be done. There is so much more offered in these courses, they gave me instruction that helped me open my business in San Diego, California Gun Aid LLC."

— GREGORY N STUEVER SR., SPRING VALLEY CA

"The theory of design, function, repair was easy for me to comprehend and worth every penny. It is such a rewarding trade and my customer base has grown exponentially. I even have other businesses that send their customers to me."

— BRIAN DAVIDSON, JANESVILLE IA

"I started Longbow Custom Firearms LLC last October. Since then, I have worked it part time, it is doing well. The biggest reason is the confidence the AGI courses have given me, to do things I would never have tried before. The design and function knowledge I have gained is priceless. My college training was as a mechanical engineer. Four years of college did not give me the same level of insight in to mechanics that over 100 hours of quality video time with AGI and Mr. Dunlap did. Again, thank you for all your help." Sincerely,

— MIKE BLAKESMITH

"I thoroughly enjoyed learning gunsmithing. It has been a lifelong desire. I undertook a course years ago, that was not as detailed or informative as AGI. As a result I never completed it. AGI's course is well presented with details that allows the student to truly understand the weapons being taught."

— KIP W HEIMENDINGER, CRAWFORDSVILLE IN

"The breadth of firearms covered in the courses is incredible, almost overwhelming. During the course, it is fascinating to see the many different mechanisms that have been created. Bob does a great job of explaining the Design, Function, and Repair of the widely varying implementations, while also pointing out where there are similarities that can help the student understand more deeply. I was fortunate to have access to many of the firearms that were used as key example of a type (e.g. Browning A-5, 1911, Winchester 94), and strongly recommend this as a valuable addition to the video information. Non-firearm components of the course are also important, and are very well done, creating a well-rounded student with all the skills necessary to begin the craft of Professional Gunsmithing. Regards,

— ROB PORTER

"This course is the best thing I've seen, I had no doubts it would be, as I have purchased a few videos from AGI in the past. But don't fool your self thinking this is just some other guy talking about guns, oh no, Mr. Dunlap goes into such great details and even repeats a lot of the more important aspects. A true Gunsmith and teacher he is, even though he's very straight forward, he also made me laugh sometimes, it was great. Ken Brooks, is another great teacher, even though he worked under Mr. Dunlap, he has his own ways of teaching which are as equally great. I wouldn't hesitate in telling or even recommending the AGI schooling or videos to anyone I come into contact with.

I just finished the last revolver video last night and signed up to start the test, I am looking forward to the shotgun section which is next. It›s not hard to lose yourself in watching these videos as they are in great detail and I really enjoy them. Thanks."

— JOSEPH WAIBEL III

**From the "Gun Surgeon's" Website:**

"Why Us? (We repair and customize firearms) As taught to us by the Premier Gunsmithing Institute in America, (American Gunsmithing Institute) and by some of the best gunsmiths America has ever known such as Robert "Bob" Dunlap, Gene Shuey, Darrell Holland to name a few, we believe in good ole' fashioned and true gunsmithing!

We start by identifying the root cause (the actual problem not the symptom) and fixing it the right way. We do not just start swapping out parts to see what works like most "gunsmith" shops do now days as that is not only costly to you the customer but it is not true gunsmithing!

Swapping out/replacing the parts can also potentially destroy the value of the gun if someone does not know what they are doing. Potentially ruining your treasured family heirloom!

We do not take shortcuts. We always go above and beyond and we can assure you that you will be satisfied with our work. We have spent a lot of time and money to learn the right way to repair firearms which does not involve just swapping out parts until it works again. If you want your firearm repaired right give us a shot! We want to earn your business and most importantly your trust and respect and we will work very hard to do so! You have our word on that!"

"PS: We are very proud that our youngest son Robert has joined us as a Gunsmithing Apprentice. Robert is also attending AGI so he too will one day soon be a fully trained, tested and certified Gunsmith so we may better serve you." Respectfully,

— MARK & SYLVIA MILLS

"Thank you for the follow up calls to make sure all is going well with receiving the course material. I have just started the introduction videos and am already learning new things. I have been a gun guy for over 30 years, so it is fun to learn new things right away. I can see that Bob is a great teacher and does an excellent job helping you understand how the different systems work. Looking forward to the learning more throughout the course."  — GARY HOLT

"I'm writing to give you my perspective on the program, now that I'm well into it. I've completed the Pro Level 1 course, including introduction to gunsmithing, pistols, shotguns, rim-fire and rifles, and have moved on to the Master course. To date, I've completed the heat-treating course, the welding course as well as the Certified Glocksmith course as part of the Master Level program. The course so far has been outstanding in that it has really challenged me to absorb all the information, yet has been presented in a manner that appeals to common sense. While my aerospace engineering background has instilled a level of critical thinking in problem solving, the AGI coursework has definitely honed those skills that have been dulled over the years.

The volume of information that Bob, Ken, Gene, and the other instructors impart instills a confidence that I will be able to tackle any general Gunsmithing repair problem that comes my way. More importantly, the design, function, and repair methodology is instilled and reinforced repeatedly as each firearm is discussed, such that the type of firearm almost becomes irrelevant as you become more and more accustomed to identifying the systems and subsystems, how they are supposed to function, and then establishing corrective action to repair the gun.

In fact, in the later sections of the courses, there were several instances where I found myself identifying the issues and corrective actions right along with Bob, which was very reassuring. As far as interactions with the AGI staff, I have had nothing but positive experiences. Everyone has been very helpful and has worked with me to get enrolled, set up my testing, as well as periodic check-ins to see how I'm doing. As I work to finish the Master program and get my shop running this year and next, I hope to take advantage of the in-person training certificates to learn even more from the instructors and take my gunsmith education to an even higher level. The AGI course has provided me with the means to pursue a lifelong dream of being a professional gunsmith and working for myself."

— T. SCARBERRY, HUNTSVILLE, AL

"I want to thank you for having a professional course on gunsmithing. I was a armorer in the US Army where I started my interest in repairing weapons. You course went into more detail and explained why and how to make repairs to weapons. Making them more dependable and affordable to repair. I have also received my FFL license the first time around by using your instructor's guidance. Thank You for doing a great job in benefiting the US veterans of America in helping their dreams come true."

— S. MICHAEL WILLIAMS

"Just got done watching a couple more hours on the pistols Gun-smithing Section, damn there is definitely more to them than I really anticipated. I really enjoy how in depth Mr. Dunlap goes into Every aspect and how to fix all kinds of issues."  — JOSEPH WAIBEL

"The materials in the course were very informative and instructive in a manner of not only how to perform various tasks but also as to WHY those tasks needed to be done. Very comprehensive courses and curriculum."  — DANNY WILLARD, NACOGDOCHES TX

"Greatest classes ever."  — ANTONE R CARRIER, CLACKAMAS, OR

"The program provides excellent history, background and Theory. Everything needed to do hands on Gunsmithing."

— ALAN INCAO, HILLSBOROUGH TOWNSHIP, NJ

"After completion of the American Gunsmithing Institute courses, I obtained my FFL and opened up a standalone gunsmith shop. I have been open now for over 10 years and provide services to customers as far away as NY. My business name is WRG Gunsmithing."

— WILLIAM GOLLEHON, ALBEMARBLE NC

# AUTHOR BIO

Gene Wayne Kelly is the founder and president of the American Gunsmithing Institute and a thought leader in trade skills education and distance education. He is radically challenging and changing the way trade skills are taught today. Including; Plumbing, Electrical, Welding, Locksmithing, Carpentry, Gunsmithing, Masonry and Tile, using the Accelerated Training Institute's proprietary online training process. Which can be combined with ATI's exclusive mobile "pop-up" Express Campuses, resulting in 30 to 90 day training to work cycles.

Gene is a Serial Entrepreneur, Educator, Published Book Author (The College Myth, why you should Not go to college if you want to be successful www.TheCollegeMyth.com), Licensed 07 Contractor, Classically trained Certified Gunsmith, FFL License holder with SOT, Direct Marketing Expert, Business Success Coach, and Board Certified Protection Professional (CPP).

He is also the proprietor of Kelly Family Vineyards, an award-winning vineyard and winery in the Napa Valley.

Gene is passionate about business and helping others succeed. He has started several successful businesses.

Mr. Kelly is a CPP, and has worked internationally as a Security Consultant and Trainer in high risk environments in association with International Security and Defense Systems (ISDS) of Israel, since 1986.

Bob Dunlap with former students from left Mark Foster, Jack Landis, AGI President Gene Kelly, at one of our GCA member Bashes about 10 years ago.

# A SPECIAL THANKS

**Bob Dunlap**
**The Master Gunsmith**
**1938—2019**

Bob Dunlap was my instructor, mentor and our AGI *Sensei* "Master Gunsmithing Instructor" who developed the "Design, Function, and Repair" teaching method for AGI. He created so many successful gunsmiths. These courses emphasize understanding firearm systems, sub-systems and the fundamentals that apply to their proper functioning.

As our Senior Instructor Robert "Bob" Dunlap was a widely respected authority in the firearms industry. He enrolled in the Lassen Gunsmithing program in 1959 and ultimately returned after operating his own successful gun shop, to became the head instructor where he completely rebuilt and reinvented how Gunsmithing was taught. Bob was the senior instructor at Lassen College Gunsmithing School for over 35 years and simultaneously operated a gunsmithing business which he determined was necessary to keep abreast of the latest developments in the Firearms industry. At one point, he employed 9 gunsmiths at his company, PISCO (Pacific International Service Company). Numerous firearms manufacturers contracted their warranty work with PISCO due to their top-notch reputation.

As a tribute to his abilities, many of his Gunsmithing students have gone on to fame within the industry. Bob's closest student and former business partner, is AGI Instructor Ken Brooks. Formerly a student of Bob Dunlap's at Lassen College and later a full-time instructor at the same Gunsmithing School they operated PISCO together for many years, until ultimately Ken took over the entire business.

After his teaching career, Bob worked with Gene Kelly to preserve and transfer all of his Design, Function, and Repair training system along with other knowledge, into a comprehensive course taught using video instruction and home study programing, to preserve the Gunsmithing Arts and teach the next generation of gunsmiths.

Besides hundreds of hours of AGI video courses, Bob appears in multiple segments of the GCA monthly video magazine "GunTech" and was an expert witness in firearm function/ malfunction cases. Bob has passed, but is not forgotten as the next generation of gunsmith as still learning at his feet through the American Gunsmithing Institute.

# GUNSMITH'S
# RESOURCE LIST

## Gun Parts -New, Used, and Surplus

Sarco Inc.
50 Hilton Street
Easton, PA 18042
(610) 250-3960
https://www.sarcoinc.com

Numrich Gun Parts Corp.
226 Williams Ln.
Kingston, NY 12401
(866) 686-7424
https://www.gunpartscorp.com

Jack First Inc.
1201 Turbine Dr.
Rapid City SD 57703
(605) 343-8481
https://jack-first-gun-parts.mys-
hopify.com

The Dealers Showroom
553 Market Street
Klamath Falls, OR 97601
(541) 882-4249
Email: johnd.bush@yahoo.com

Old Western Scrounger
54 Dupont Rd.
Martinsburg, WV
(304) 274-0004
www.ows-ammo.com

Midwest Gun Works
1101 Mason Circle Drive
Pevely, MO 63070
(636) 475-7300
www.midwestgunworks.com

Old Arms of Idaho
4910 W. Denton Street
Boise, ID 83706
OldArmsofidaho.com
(208) 602-6027

Popperts Gun Parts
P.O. Box 413
Glenside, PA 19038
(215) 887-2391
www.poppertsgunparts.com/order.
htm

Gun Grip Supply
TEAD Inc
PO Box 162
Mineral Springs NC 28108
(980) 277-4301
www.gungripsupply.com

**AR/1911 Parts and Accessories**

JSE Surplus
5004 State Highway 74
Cape Girardeau MO 63701
(866) 833 7177
www.jsesurplus.com

JoeBobOutfitters
4850 General Hays Rd
Hays, KS 67601
(785) 639-7121
www.joeboboutfitters.com

Primary Arms
3219 South Sam Houston Parkway
East, Ste 100

Houston, Texas 7704
(713) 344-9600
www.primaryarms.com

Palmetto State Armory
3760 Fernandina Rd.
Columbia, SC 29210
(803) 551-2680
www.palmettostatearmory.com

Wing Tactical
280 S. Lemon Avenue #812
Walnut, CA 91788
(909) 444-0240
www.wingtactical.com
CDNN Sports
(800) 588-9500
www.cdnnsports.com

Gun Mag Warehouse
631 Southwestern Blvd. Suite 140
Coppell, TX 75019
(800) 409-9439
www.gunmagwarehouse.com/

**Gunsmithing Tools**

Brownells
Gun Tools, Parts, Supplies, Shooting accessories
200 South Front Street,
Montezuma, Iowa 50171
(800) 741-0015
www.brownells.com

Midway USA
Gun Tools, Parts, Supplies, Shooting accessories
5875 West Van Horn Tavern Road
Columbia, MO 65203-9274
(800) 243-3220
www.midwayusa.com

**Gunsmithing Training**

AGI – American Gunsmithing
Institute/Gunsmithing Club of
America
351 2nd Street
Napa, CA 94559
(800) 797-0867 or 707-253-0462
www.americangunsmith.com

Gunsmithing Club of America
www.GunsmithingClubofAmer-
ica.com

**Refinishing Materials and
Systems**

DU-LITE Corp.
Chemicals for: Hot Caustic
Bluing, Black Oxide, Post 64
Winchester Bluing, Parkerizing,
Etc.
71 River Road
Middletown, CT 06457
(860) 347-2505
www.du-lite.com

NIC Industries
Cerakote (Spray-on,
Bake-on finishes)
7050 Sixth Street
White City, OR 97503
(866) 774-7628
www.cerakote.com

H&M Metal Processing
Black Nitride Coating
1414 Kenmore Blvd
Akron, Ohio 44314
6051 N. 56th Avenue
Glendale, Az 85301
(330) 745-3075
www.blacknitride.com

Lauer Custom Weaponry
DuraCoat
3601 129th St.
Chippewa Falls, WI 54729
(800) 830-6677
www.duracoatfirearmfinishes.com

**Barrels & Blanks**

Lilja
High End Barrels and Blanks
P.O. Box 372
Plains, Montana 59859
(406) 826-3084
riflebarrels.com/support/
contact-us/

Shilen Rifles, Inc.
2501 North Interstate Highway 45
Ennis, Texas, USA 75119
(972) 875-5318
www.shilen.com

Douglas Barrels Incorporated
5504 Big Tyler Road
Charleston, Wv 25313-1398
(304) 776 1341

Green Mountain Rifle Barrel Co.
PO BOX 2670
153 West Main St
Conway, NH 03818
(603) 447-1095
www.gmriflebarrel.com

E. R. Shaw
5312 Thoms Run Road
Bridgeville, PA 15017
(412) 221-3636
www.shawcustombarrels.com

## Stocks

Macon Gunstocks
Walnut and Laminate Blanks,
Semi-Fit, Duplicating, Checkering
and Finishing
34535 Lickingteller Ave
Warsaw, MO 65355
(660) 438-4697

Boyd's Hardwood Stocks
25376 403rd Avenue
Mitchell, SD 57301

(605) 996-5011
https://www.boydsgunstocks.com

Stocky's
Many Different Brands and
In-House Stocks
3748 Prospect Ave Unit #1
West Palm Beach, FL 33404
(561) 584-8500
https://www.stockysstocks.com

McMillan
1638 W. Knudsen Dr., Suite 101
Phoenix, AZ 85027
(877) 365.6148
www.mcmillanusa.com

Bell & Carlson
101 Allen Road
Dodge City, KS 67801
(620) 225-6688
www.bellandcarlson.com

Magpul Industries
8226 Bee Caves Rd
Austin, TX 78746
(877) 462-4785
www.magpul.com

H-S Precision
1301 Turbine Dr.
Rapid City, SD 57703
(605) 341-3006
www.hsprecision.com

## Triggers

Timney Triggers
2020 West Quail Ave.
Phoenix, AZ 85027
(866) 484-6639
wwww.timneytriggers.com

Geissle Automatics
800 North Wales Road
North Wales, PA 19454
(610) 272–2060
www.geissele.com
Apex Tactical Specialties
8009 W. Olive Avenue
Peoria, AZ 85345
(623) 322-0200
www.apextactical.com

Kidd Innovative Design
(World's Best 10/22 Triggers)
2633 Terminal Loop Rd.
McQueeney, TX. 78123
(830) 557-5433
www.kiddinnovativedesign.com/

# ACKNOWLEDGEMENTS

My Mom and Dad, Harold and Betty Kelly who encouraged me all through life and made sacrifices to enable me to explore my unusual path to success.

Master Gunsmith Bob Dunlap, my instructor and *Sensei* who developed the Design, Function, and Repair teaching process and was grumpily willing to teach the entire system on video. What he shared has changed countless lives for the better.

Keith Hezmalhalch our video producer who put up with a ton of crap from the instructors and managed to coach the very best from them anyway, so that we have been able to preserve the real Gunsmithing Arts, all the while doing it on a shoe string.

Mark Foster and Darrell Holland, the other two members of the Lassen College Gunsmithing school "Three Musketeers" and lifelong true friends, who helped me succeed in school, both of whom are Gunsmiths extraordinaire and who have also shared their personal expertise with our students.

Don Farmer, my welding instructor who first pointed me in the direction of Gunsmithing and who demonstrated to me that "laws and rules were just strong suggestions!" Maybe that is why I tend to color outside the lines.

Our American Gunsmithing Institute Gunsmithing instructors who have freely shared their decades of personal experience and expertise to educate and enhance the lives of tens of thousands of Gunsmiths and Firearm Enthusiasts around the World: Gene Shuey, Jack Landis, Ken Brooks, Darrell Holland, Mark Foster, John D. Bush, Fred Zeglin, Robert Dunn, T.R. Graham, Bob Rizzetto, Chris Andre, and many others including the Grand Master, Bob Dunlap.

The entire staff of the American Gunsmithing Institute who have enabled us to pursue the mission of preserving the Gunsmithing Arts and helped our students become successful Gunsmiths World-wide.

My wife Paula and son Jacob who have traveled with me on this journey and have actively supported the effort, to the point that Jacob M. Kelly is now Director of AGI Operations, carrying on the tradition.

The Lord Jesus Christ, the Holy Spirit, and God the Father whom have provided me with the grace and opportunity to make a living doing what I have loved for over a quarter century and counting. Thank you Lord!

American
Gunsmithing
Institute

To become a Certified Professional Gunsmith, contact:

American Gunsmithing Institute

351 Second Street, Napa, CA. 94559

1-800-797-0867

**www.AmericanGunsmithingInstitute.com**

For FREE Gunsmithing Mini lessons and
Video Armorer's Courses on your specific firearms, contact:
**www.AmericanGunsmith.com**

1-800-797-0867

To join a community of like minded individuals, go to:

The Gunsmithing Club of America

**www.GunsmithingClubofAmerica.com**

Gunsmithing Student Success Stories:

**www.AgiReviews.com**